FLEET & CROOKHAM
A Pictorial History

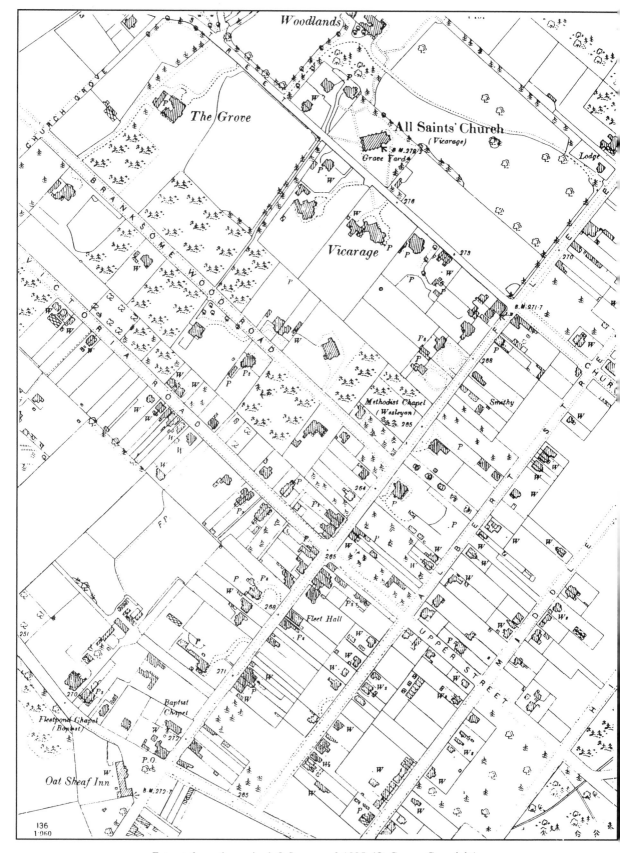

Extract from the revised O.S. map of 1895 (© Crown Copyright).

FLEET & CROOKHAM
A Pictorial History

Stan Knight, Peter Pimm,
Percy Vickery & Tony Wright

Phillimore

1994

Published by
PHILLIMORE & CO. LTD.,
Shopwyke Manor Barn, Chichester, West Sussex

ISBN 0 85033 926 X

Printed and bound in Great Britain by
BIDDLES LTD.
Guildford, Surrey

List of Illustrations

Frontispiece: O.S. map, 1895

Acknowledgements

We should like to thank many people for their help, particularly Noel Osborne, Managing Director of Phillimore for suggesting the book in the first place and Yvonne Wyatt, Archivist of the Fleet and Crookham Local History Group for typing the introduction and captions and for providing a chapter on Church Crookham. In addition, thanks go to Chris Hall for his contribution to the text on Fleet Pond.

Photographs and text were kindly provided by the following, and their assistance is gratefully acknowledged: Mrs. J. Ainley; Mrs. E. Beale; Mr. E. Brothers; Mrs. Q. Davies; The Francis Frith Collection; Dr. J. Garland; Mrs. C. Heathers; Mr. G. Hoar; Mrs. Jolly; Miss H. Knapman; Mr. R. Mitten; Mr. H. H. Pool; Mr. M. S. Smith; Mr. D. R. F. Tapp; Mr. D. White; Fleet Baptist Church; Hampshire Record Office, Winchester; Ordnance Survey, Southampton; R.A.M.C. Museum, Mytchett; Rural Life Museum, Tilford; St Nicholas School.

Any errors and omissions remain the sole responsibility of the co-editors.

PETER PIMM
STAN KNIGHT
PERCY VICKERY
TONY WRIGHT

Foreword

The history of the area in north-east Hampshire, which today we know as Fleet and Crookham, has been determined to a large degree by the underlying geology. From the outcrop of the Upper Chalk south of Crondall, a series of Tertiary deposits are exposed, which form the outer rim of the London and Thames basins, and the streams flow northwards.

Heavy clays of the London and Bracklesham series occur to the south and the yellow and golden sands of the Bagshot beds lie to the north. The town centre of Fleet has its foundations on a comparatively level spread of plateau gravel laid down by a north-flowing river in geologically recent prehistoric times.

There is a significant change in scenery coincident with the boundary of the Bracklesham and Bagshot beds. This is observed quite clearly on the ground at the line of demarcation between Crookham Village and Church Crookham/Fleet.

The whole of the area under review formed the tithing of Crokeham within the Hundred of Crondall, which itself occupied a large area of north-east Hampshire. It was bounded by the counties of Berkshire and Surrey to the north, Alton Hundred to the south and Odiham and Holdshott Hundreds to the west.

The hamlet of Crookham (now Crookham Village) evolved in Saxon times coincidentally with Crondall, on good but heavy agricultural land bordering the tiny River Hart. It used the mill only a few yards over the western border at Pilcot. To the north lay an almost uninterrupted expanse of heathland, Crookham Common, part of the Great Heath which extended, and still does, across the county boundaries to the north and east.

To the north of the Common a tributary of the Hart was dammed to form Fleet Pond and another mill provided for a pocket of agricultural land. It is from this area that the present name of the town derives.

It is for the relevant chapters of this book to relate, how in the 19th century, largely due to transport improvements and the foundation of the military Aldershot, first Crookham, and then Fleet became separate parishes, and eventually Fleet and Church Crookham an Urban District.

Introduction

This brief introduction to the pictorial history of Fleet and Crookham begins with Fleet Pond because of its early influence on the development of the area. Then follows Crookham Village and ultimately Fleet and Church Crookham.

Fleet Pond

Though of somewhat obscure origin, there has been conjecture that Fleet Pond was man-made during the Roman occupation. The Saxons allegedly named the pond 'Fugelmere' (wild fowl pond). During the Middle Ages a pasture close by was named 'Le Flete', a name subsequently applied to all of the general area, including the two ponds existing then.

Evidence of these ponds as an important source of fish is given in the records of Crondall Manor, where we read of expenditure by the Priory and Convent of St Swithin's at Winchester for repairs to sluices, nets and boats. We may imagine that from the 13th to the 15th centuries Winchester directly 'managed' the ponds, possibly with locally based monks. Oral tradition speaks of monks at a grange, in what is today Velmead Road, to look after the ponds.

1   This view shows about half of the smaller section of The Lake, or Fleet Pond as it is known, *c*.1910. It has always been in private ownership, whereas the larger area was for a century in WD/MOD hands. A favourite watering place in horse transport days, the soldiers here are most probably artillery men from Leipzig Barracks, Ewshot, which housed a brigade of Royal Field Artillery (R.F.A.) at that time.

The ponds seem to have been divided by some kind of causeway—called 'Le Fletebrygge'—which possibly carried a road of some importance, perhaps Cove Road, given the often repeated requirement to keep it in good condition.

By the 15th century the Prior was leasing the pasture and fishing rights to several local adjacent owners, but required a token supply of 100 fish to Winchester on feast days. Perhaps the monks had found a more convenient source of fish, and wished to disengage themselves from the direct work. In any event, logistical factors may have been particularly significant, given the distance and therefore the journey time between Fleet and Winchester.

Indeed, even for such a small amount as 100 fish the wording of some of the leases suggests that this was a niggling issue. For example, the 1491 lease stated that 'fish should be caught and carried with great care' to the Priory; later, in 1505, the lease required that 'fish be carried and delivered in a good and fresh state'.

The monks had effectively transferred to others a commercial undertaking requiring only the 100 fish and an annual rent of 23 shillings. The clientele, other than the local population of Crondall and Itchell Manors, may also have included Odiham Castle, and perhaps the nuns at nearby Wintney Priory.

For such a venture to be viable, the infrequent but major fishing would probably have involved lowering the water level, using seine nets with boats and, following the catch, sorting the fish by size and type to stew ponds. Although such small fish ponds are marked on 19th-century maps in the Court Moor and Dinorben areas of Fleet, it cannot be assumed for certain that these same ponds existed in the later Middle Ages.

From 1558 a new lease ended the requirement to supply the 100 fish, but compensated the Priory by increasing the annual rent by 20s. (one pound). Shortly after, in 1567, the situation changed again, when a severe storm swept away the retaining banks of one of the ponds. Repairs would have been costly, so instead permission was granted to convert the site to pasture and meadow.

The location of the lost pond has bred two opposing theories: the one placing it to the north of the surviving pond on what is now Ancells Park, the other, proposing the south as more probable, and citing the name 'Pondtail' as supporting evidence. Last century, there existed a Pondtail Farm south of Fleet Pond. An ancient moated stew pond was situated about one mile south-west of the pond.

The landscape of 200 years ago would be unfamiliar and unrecognisable to us today. Fleet Pond was a lake amid a vast tract of heathland and peatmoors. In the 1680s John Aubrey visited Frimley, and wrote of a 'vast heathy country'. He added, 'Here is a great Pond, called Fleet Pond, remarkable for its biggness', though he was unsure if the boundaries of Frimley parish extended to it.

In the 18th and 19th centuries the enclosure movement gathered momentum. Hawley Common was enclosed in 1817 and Crookham Common by 1834. The Hawley enclosure included all of the heathland between Southwood and Fleet Pond; Crookham Common abutted the pond on its west and south sides, and covered all of the land which is now the town of Fleet and Church Crookham.

Enclosure allowed the gentry to divide and develop the commons as they saw fit. Their opportunities multiplied on 7 April 1836, when the London and Southampton Railway Company purchased, for £50, 'the Fleet Mill Pond and certain allotments of wasteland (i.e. heathland of the former commons) belonging to Fleet Farm'. The railway was laid on an embankment straight across the Pond, separating a small northern section (known as Fleet Little Pond) from the larger southern section.

The Pond quickly proved a popular attraction, and the railway company built an additional station named Fleet Pond and provided special excursions from London. The vicinity was ripe for development and a new settlement, at first called Fleet Pond, later Fleet itself, began to grow.

The larger section of the pond, meanwhile, became part of the new military estate attached to Aldershot camp, and remained under the jurisdiction of the Army from 1854 to 1972. They were to use it for all manner of exercises and experiments, including creating four islands, testing early designs of hydroplanes and establishing a summer camp on the heathland east of the pond.

Within a decade or so of the opening of the railway, Fleet Pond began to attract an army of an altogether different kind, namely many Victorian naturalists, and references to its wild flowers in particular are frequent in natural history journals of the last century. Among the rarities they sought were marsh gentian, marsh orchids and the pale heath violet. None of these, alas, grows there today.

Fleet Pond was a focus for social life in the town. In winter when it froze, sometimes for weeks, hundreds of people gathered there for ice skating and games such as curling or ice hockey. In summer there were picnics in the Sandhills (banks of silver sand amongst the heather on the east side, now all overgrown), games on the beach and bathing where the water was deep enough. The War Department did not allow public boating until about 1910.

In 1940 the pond was drained, to prevent its use by enemy aircraft as a navigational aid. During the war years willow scrub grew up across the bed, and prisoners of war were put to work to clear this before the pond was refilled.

The pond has retained its reputation as a haven for wildlife, and this was formally recognised in 1951 when it became one of the first Sites of Special Scientific Interest to be designated in Hampshire. The reasons for this accolade were the importance of the lake to waterfowl, its extensive area (Fleet Pond is the largest freshwater lake in Hampshire) and the great variety of wetland and heathland flowers.

2 This view of Little Pond was taken from the old Cove Road looking towards Fleet Station, in the 1950s. It shows clearly 'The Lido', constructed as part of Fleet Country Club in the 1930s. Open to the public, it was the only such facility in the Urban District and was used for swimming lessons by the pupils of Fleet schools.

Crookham Village

Crookham Village is the ancient hamlet formerly at the heart of an extensive tything of the Saxon parish of Crondall. The tything encompassed all that area now known as Fleet and Church Crookham. It probably owes its existence to the tiny River Hart and to the mill at Pilcot just over the border with Dogmersfield.

Crookham, despite its Saxon name, is not mentioned in Domesday Book perhaps because it formed part of the Manor of Crondall. However, there are many medieval mentions where the spelling is usually Crocham or Crokeham, e.g. in the Compotus de Crondal, this being an account of the Manor rendered to the Prior at Winchester. On 28 September 1248 it mentions on the debit side '2s. 1d. to Blakeman de Crokeham for his feudal services released yearly' and on the credit side '13s. 4d. from the tything of Crockham that they may be in the Lords liberty'. (These costs are given in old shillings and pence.) The Crondall Customary of 1567 sought to regularise the land holdings, which had become chaotic following the Dissolution of the Priory and the transfer of the Manor to the Bishop of Winchester. This Customary, besides being a written statement of usual or habitual practice including rents and holdings, gives a most interesting list of places and surnames. Some of them are recognisable today.

The Basingstoke Canal, which opened in 1794, the Crookham and Ewshott Enclosure Act of 1829, the coming of the railway to Shapley Heath (now Winchfield) in 1836, and to Fleet Pond a little later, and subsequently the establishment of the great army camp at Aldershot, all had a profound effect on the tything. Because of squatters on the Common and later development following enclosure, Crookham became a separate parish in 1840 and Christ Church was consecrated in 1841. Though the ancient village is now a separate civil parish, it is still a part of the ecclesiastical parish.

Twenty years later, due to influences already mentioned, the area once known as Fleet Pond was created a separate parish and later in 1904 became an Urban District. As a consequence of the Local Government Reorganisation of 1932 it was proposed that Crookham should be amalgamated with the Urban District as a separate ward. In the event only the area known as Church Crookham was considered to be of sufficient rateable value to be included in the new ward. Crookham Village (or Crookham Street as it was then known) became a ward of the civil parish of Crondall. This situation continued until well after the Second World War. In less than a decade the population doubled, due to scattered infilling of private dwellings and a fair number of Local Government houses. In 1952 a number of public spirited folk petitioned for the creation of a separate civil parish and this was granted.

The old village centre, now a conservation area, has retained its character. Though housing estates which adjoin the border with Fleet and Church Crookham have increased the population to over 3,000, for postal purposes they are in Church Crookham.

The geological boundary between the clay farmland of the old village and the former commonland is quite distinct. The pines and heather of Fleet and Church Crookham give way to oak, ash and hazel coppices and fertile ploughland. The clay subsoil is also responsible for former local industries of pottery and brickmaking. A brick and tile works existed at Zephon Common and there was a pottery in Crookham Street and another at Grove Farm. Many of the bricks for the 18th-century Basingstoke Canal bridges were made locally.

The soil was also very suitable for growing hops and at least four hop kilns existed. One of these, now converted to another industrial purpose, was in use until 1974 to process the

3   The Malthouse, Crookham Village, now known as 'Brunley', a single residence, at present screened by trees. The building was, at the time of the photograph *c*.1910, a terrace of farmworkers' cottages. It is of 17th-century origin and would originally have comprised the maltster's home and business premises. The trade is recalled in the names of the nearby Malthouse Bridge and Malthouse Close.

4   Hill House, Crookham Village, was a large residence owned by Mr. Nissen. The photograph of his Argyle car and chauffeur, Mr. Lambert, was taken *c*.1913, and his car was believed to be the first one owned by a village resident. The black arm band may have been worn for Col. Forde, the previous owner of Hill House, who died there in 1912.

5 The *Black Horse*, Crookham Village, has been in business for at least 150 years and has changed surprisingly little since this early 20th-century picture was taken. The landlord, James Ayres, is probably in the pony trap, whilst the lady in the doorway is almost certainly Mrs. Ayres. Thomas Kenward of Hartley Wintney, the brewer referred to on the sign, sold the business in 1921.

last crop grown on Grove Farm. It is very distinctive with its twin slatted pyramidal towers and hipped ventilators. Perhaps more unusually, tobacco was grown locally at Redfields in the early part of this century, the only location in Britain to produce this crop commercially.

Ancient dwellings along Crookham Street formed the basis of the village. Most of the timber-framed buildings are probably 17th century, although parts of Grove Farm House are undoubtedly of Tudor origin. Two Ponds Cottage, the last house before the boundary with Crondall, is of cruck construction, one of the most westerly in England, and of a much earlier medieval date. Lavender Cottage dates from between 1620 and 1650, confirmed by a wall mural discovered by the former residents. The painting may have commemorated a marriage or birth, showing the initials MH, PH and WH. Brook House, a brick edifice with a Dutch gable dated 1664, is the gem of the village, said to be one wing of a larger building, and is the subject of local legends of royal visits.

The Hearth Tax Returns of 1665 listed no less than 43 households in Crookham accounting for 107 hearths, with a further 24 hearths not chargeable—rather more than Aldershot at the same time.

Other buildings of interest include the *Chequers Inn*, Crondall Road, an 18th-century brick structure with a slate roof, which reportedly held the first contract for boarding canal employees and horses and, as with other nearby inns, had close associations with the Basingstoke Canal. The 18th-century Canal Cottage in Crondall Road formerly was the canal wharfinger's office and cottage.

An ancient Mummers play is performed in the village on Boxing Day, most of the characters dressed in strips of paper and declaiming a death and resurrection plot which may well be a survival from early medieval Crusader days.

Fleet

Fleet did not develop because of a single factor: there were no mineral deposits requiring labour, no benefactor setting up a factory nor even an historical context around which the town could grow. Fleet's development lay in a combination of related aspects, the Pond and its recreational potential, the railway and access to and from London and the proximity of 'the Royal Camp', as the army camp was known in 1856, at Aldershot.

Early house literature extolled the virtue of the area, typically 'the healthy and rapidly improving neighbourhood of Fleet' (1877); 'a proverbially healthy and favourite residential district' (1886) and 'Fleet, famous for its pretty sylvan scenery and the health-giving properties of the pines that abound ...' (1916). By 1859, a directory listed villas, tradesmen and hostelries such as *The Oat Sheaf*, as being at Fleet Pond, the name of the early locality, with a post office close by. In 1862, Rose Farm Dairy was established by Mark Kimber, although it was then known as Rose Cottage Farm Dairy.

The ancient system of commonland was slowly but steadily eroded as the population grew. As the commons were enclosed, commoners lost their centuries-old rights to graze cattle, sheep or ponies, cut peat for fuel or cut heather, bracken and gorse. The last peat to be cut in the area was from commonland behind the *Foresters Inn*. Early maps of the time show scattered houses across the area generally west of Fleet Road and also strung along Reading Road South. By 1871, the population of Fleet was still only 380.

This picture was to change significantly in 1878 when H. J. Brake, a land agent from Farnborough, acquired the land between the east side of Fleet Road and down to the Basingstoke Canal from the estate of Thomas Keep. In 1880 he set out a road network with

6 A double wedding, 1898. The two brides were sisters, maiden name Yeomans, whose family lived in Cove. The bride and groom just right of centre are Kate (Yeomans) and William James Wright, whose father was George Wright, the miller at Fleet Mill. William himself became the headmaster of Crookham School in Gally Hill Road (1905-25).

building plots in grid arrangement parallel with Fleet Road. The result of the ensuing sale of land was to see Fleet grow significantly in the late 19th century and in turn encourage the influx of trades and commercial activity to make the town increasingly self-sufficient.

In 1862 All Saints was consecrated as the first Church of England church in the town, establishing Fleet as a separate ecclesiastical parish. The church was built by Mr. Lefroy, who reputedly made the bricks at the brickworks at Bourley, near the large reservoir.

For their part Baptists worshipped initially in a house called Hope House off Reading Road North and subsequently at Hope Chapel which adjoined the then 'dissenters' own burying ground near Victoria Road. A second small chapel was erected called Ebenezer Chapel near the Oatsheaf crossroads. Subsequently, because of the inadequacy of these chapels, a new Baptist Chapel was built in 1892 with a seating capacity for 200 people.

In the same period All Saints used Fleetbrook Mission, positioned on the Cove Road, for services for those living near to Fleet Pond.

The Methodist Church developed strongly in Fleet and, following successful outdoor meetings by visiting preachers, the need for a permanent meeting place was satisfied when a timber chapel was built in 1887 in Branksomewood Road. This became too small for the congregation in 1899 and in 1900 a Wesleyan Methodist Church was constructed close by.

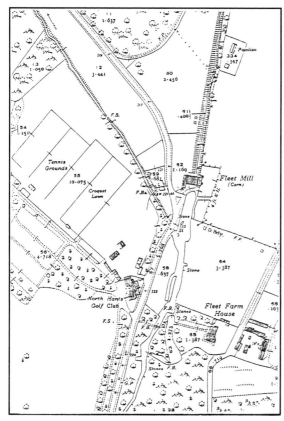

In 1889 Capital and Counties (later Lloyds) Bank opened a branch in Fleet Road since, by 1891, the population had risen to 1,067. It was to double in the following decade.

In the ten-year period between 1894 and 1904, a parish council was established in 1894, and Fleet Cottage Hospital was opened in 1897. The railway through Fleet Station was enlarged to four tracks instead of two, and the new station opened. In 1904 the area was uprated to urban district status, a designation which continued until the reorganisation of 1974.

Such was the extent of growth that by 1916 recreational opportunities nearby were many, including golf, a cricket club and hunting with the Garth, Hampshire Hunt, Vine and Aldershot Drag hounds. The cricket club was reported in 1896 to have a large membership. Race meetings were held three times a year on nearby Tweseldown Hill. In the 1920s, a hockey club was formed, and the members rented part of the cricket club's pitch on which to build the hockey field. A polo club was also formed, with their clubhouse and field at Ancells Farm, near Fleet Mill.

7   Ordnance Survey map of 1939 (© Crown Copyright), printed in 1945, showing Fleet Mill with the mill stream and, to the south, Fleet Farm House. The stream divided, one part running parallel to Minley Road the other flowing past Brook House to the north. Note the pavilion and polo grounds in the top right.

8 Crested china, showing the emblem of three trees in a shield for 'Fleet' or 'Fleet, Hants'. Mr. Parnell, 186 Fleet Road, sold crockery and kitchenware and commissioned such pieces from manufacturers including Grafton, Arcadian, Clifton and W. M. Goss. In the 1920s the same crest was shown in issues of the Fleet Chamber of Commerce journals. The crest was used on the Albert Street School cap badge.

The bigger residences with their large gardens, even described as estates, were to provide ample potential for employment in service and also for diverse trades. An O.S. map of 1896 shows no fewer than nine nurseries established in Fleet alone.

Although the population in the late 19th century was still comparatively small, many social initiatives were undertaken. Fleet Hall was erected in 1891 and a little earlier in 1887 Albert Street Institute and Reading Rooms were opened with a small charge for access to morning and evening papers. A brass band of 13 members was established and was well supported.

The original small school, established in Church Road in 1860, was, by the early 1880s, unable to meet the growing population's needs. As a result the National School for boys, girls and infants situated in Albert Street was built in 1886 and it was subsequently enlarged in 1893 with a residence for the master. In 1896 the average attendance at the school was 260 children.

By 1914 and the outbreak of war, Fleet had become a small town with over 40 shops concentrated in Fleet Road and a population of around 3,000. The nearby Royal Aircraft Factory at Farnborough was built and became a source of local employment.

Fleet Road became the focal point of the town. As early as the 1860s, Ernest Oakley had built and established his department store at the junction with Upper Street to become known as Oakley's Corner. The cupola and clock tower are still in existence as a reminder of his enterprise, as is Oakley Park which was presented to the people of Fleet in 1918.

Much of the development of Fleet in this early period can be attributed to a number of local builders, including Mays, Limings, Dimes, Turners and Pools. Mr. H. J. Pool had an established family business in the early part of the century and in 1913 opened premises in Fleet Road which had a builder's yard at the rear. Immediately opposite, a saw mill was established during the war years, and it stretched through to Albert Street. In 1921 Mr. Pool purchased from the War Office a portion of Fleet Pond known as the Flash and the area was subsequently filled in. This enabled the saw mills and builder's business to be transferred. Between the 1920s and 1960s Pool and Son built almost all of the houses in Reading Road North and developed property on what is now known as the Blue Triangle.

Although still expanding, Fleet remained very much a residential area and many commuted to London for employment. However, during 1929, Ernest and Percy Tapp moved to Fleet from Balham to start the manufacture of six-wheeled vehicles, initially for use in the Smithfield and Covent Garden markets. By 1937 they had taken over for their business the old council offices, yard and adjoining fire station in Albert Street. Their engineering inventiveness was to bring a long association with the Ford Motor Company as they had developed a unique double-rear axle for the trucks and subsequently four-wheel drives for tractors. County Commercial Cars was thus established, and in the 1970s the firm dominated the four-wheel drive market for tractors; at its peak County employed over 400 staff. The business eventually closed in 1983.

For one reason or another celebrations were entered into with much gusto and carnivals also formed an important part of entertainment in the 1930s. However, it was not until the 1950s that the Fleet Carnival, as we know it today, became established. Fleet Chamber of Trade was prominent in the first carnival in 1955, now an annual summer event and still ranked as one of the best in the south of England.

Church Crookham

With the Enclosure Act of 1829, people were able to settle on land that had been protected for the use of the commoners for pasturage of their cattle and the gathering of fuel. That was to change.

The population was beginning to rise and most of the people were still concentrated in the village of Crookham, two miles or more from the parish church at Crondall. Those in the north and east were very nearly three miles away from any ecclesiastical care—and the dissenters were moving in to fill the need! Initially they met in homes, but eventually, when numbers grew, mission rooms were built. The Primitive Methodists built a 'new' church in Reading Road South in 1883, opposite Heatherside, replacing an earlier building the position of which is unknown. The Methodists used a small mission room near Crookham Crossroads which they leased to the Baptists when they themselves had acquired bigger premises.

A new parish was formed in 1840 and Christ Church was built and consecrated in 1841, and it was not long before the hamlet became known as Church Crookham. It had formerly been called Gally Hill. As well as the school (built in 1843 in Gally Hill Road), which was necessary for the growing number of children in the area, almshouses were built near the church some ten years later for the elderly and needy. The almshouses resulted from a legacy of Miss Isabella Cottrell of Bath, a sister of Mrs. Lefroy of Ewshot House.

Following the Crimean War the Government bought large tracts of land for military training purposes, which included commonland of Crookham Tything, thus depriving the

9   Sandy Lane, Church Crookham, *c*.1905. The lane lived up to its name until the mid-1920s when it was surfaced with tarmac—fortunately, despite widening the road, most of the pine trees on the left still remain. Around 1900, the War Department purchased land to the left, which today is the site of Queen Elizabeth Barracks and the home of the Gurkha Rifles.

local people of their rights of grazing, estovers and turbary. To make up the losses felt by the commoners, the Crookham and Ewshot Fuel Fund was set up by the War Department to compensate these people annually. In 1889 the interest on the Fund was £94 to be distributed among people in Crookham and Fleet.

Crossing the heathland were many tracks, but two in particular were important, crossing each other at a point now known as Crookham Crossroads. One led north to Reading (via Fleet), and the other was an east-west route from Crondall to Farnborough. An 1816 map indicates that these two tracks were well used, as the *Horns* and *North Horns* inns were well established nearby.

The arrival of the railway and Fleet Pond Station brought to this area visitors of a different kind—Londoners. Some were just looking for recreation by the Pond and in the surrounding country, others, with means, were looking for a country retreat in an attractive and healthy district. Some, no doubt, bought land as a speculation, others came and built their estates: Basingbourne in the 1860s, Dinorben Court in 1871, Court Moor later in the

10 Church Crookham crossroads, *c*.1910. It is believed that this is 'Cabby' May going about his business, plying for hire. Eighty years on, a roundabout has now been constructed to ease the congestion at this busy 'out of town' junction.

1870s occupying most of the land west of the Reading Road South, with Heatherside on the east side. In the main these people were solicitors, estate agents, auctioneers and the like, all interested in the property market in one way or another. Others buying houses were army officers, who were finding homes to settle their families.

These properties needed many people to run them; there was the domestic scene and the estate and stables had to be maintained in suitable fashion. All this new building drew in the craftsmen—brickmakers, wheelwrights and builders and the tradespeople—the shop-keepers, nurserymen, painters and decorators. Families already in the area, e.g. the Limings, took full advantage of the new prosperity, as also did the Lunns and Normans.

A small outcrop of clay gave rise to the Gally Hill Brickworks at the junction with Coxheath Road. It probably lasted only a few years around 1885, operated by Parks and Marshall, brickmakers, on land believed to have been leased from W. Cohen of Aldershot.

Other than the big estates, the main concentration of people in Church Crookham was by the church and along the Aldershot Road from the Crookham Crossroads past the *Wyvern Arms*, as it was then known, along to Ewshot Lane.

Because of the railway and the penny post, it was not long before a post office was established under the watchful eye of James Liming, who, incidentally, built Ewshot church in 1873. Wheelwrights such as the Lunns were also kept busy with the increase in traffic. These trading families proved to be both adaptable and enterprising—wherever they saw a new need they were ready to supply it. Those who were carriers dealing in coal and coke entered the furniture removal business and were responsible for the early buses and taxis of the district—again the Limings, Knights and Mays took advantage of the trade.

The big residences had their own supplies of garden produce, fruit, vegetables and flowers, but there was plenty of scope for the establishment of nurseries to supply the needs of the growing population. As was the case in Fleet, by the turn of the century there were several established in Church Crookham; in Pine Grove, for example, the Field Brothers stayed until at least the 1930s, each having an eye for the London market.

The army presence was always felt. Leipzig Barracks were built on the border with Ewshot, to house artillery returning from the South African War. Early in the First World War a hutted camp, first known as Tweseldown Camp, was built at Haig Lines. A race course was laid out over Tweseldown Hill under the control of the Army Race Committee. Not only was this useful for improving the quality of the cavalry through training but it naturally became a focus for the social events always associated with a racecourse. (Just before the Second World War the *North Horns* inn close by the course was designated a Trust House!)

More barracks were built in 1938/9 for the Royal Army Service Corps Militia—Boyce Barracks (later renamed Queen Elizabeth Barracks). This camp later became the Depot and Training Establishment of the Royal Army Medical Corps, which had been at Haig Lines, and the fine house at Redfields was used as an officers' mess in the 1940s. Queen Elizabeth Barracks, which is actually in the civil parish of Crondall (Ewshot Ward) but postally Church Crookham, is now the base for a battalion of Gurkha Rifles. The six battalions belonging to the four regiments, still part of the British Army, rotate at approximately 18-month intervals.

The social changes following the First World War were becoming evident. Girls and women were not so ready to go into 'service' if they could get a better paid job and live at home. They found regular work (but hard by today's standards) in places such as the four laundries. The men, a lot fewer now, were finding that their traditional jobs no longer existed—the car had replaced the horse. So those men with a mechanical inclination worked with firms such as Stevens Bros.

Dinorben Court, the home of the Chinnock family, London solicitors, was sold in the 1930s. For a few years it was the Stockton House Preparatory School (having had to move out of Stockton House itself), but was taken over during the war for military accommodation. Some house development had already begun near Reading Road South on what is now Dinorben Avenue.

The Figgess family of Court Moor had, early in the century, given a corner of their estate, at the Castle Street/Reading Road junction, to be used for the less fortunate by building the Court Moor Home of Rest. This was in use, evidenced by Trade Directories, initially for children, then later as a home for elderly men. It was run latterly by the Church Army and was finally sold in the late 1970s.

Court Moor House fell vacant in the 1930s. It was a long house; the centre was demolished but the two ends were incorporated in two new dwellings. The grounds of Court Moor were developed and became Courtmoor Avenue and Greenways. Court Moor School was built in the late 1950s largely on the grounds of the Dinorben estate.

The different owners of Basingbourne over the years bought up parcels of land on the east side of the Reading Road, and at the 1910 sale these parcels were described as very suitable for development. This included all the land between what is today Florence Road and Pine Grove, and interestingly referred to possible new roads including Florence Road, Queens Road and Ordnance Road. This last named road never materialised. The house was eventually let out in flats and still stands today.

Heatherside, a smaller property, surrounded by the grazing cattle of Mark Kimber's Rose Farm Dairy, remained a private residence until the 1950s when for a short while it was used as a hotel, before being demolished and Heatherside Infant School was built. Originally the Junior School of today was used as a senior school before Courtmoor was opened.

By the end of the century there was evidence of leisure activities: the rifle club and a strong horticultural association catering for the whole district. The 1892 *Fleet Reporter* records—'The annual show of the Crondall, Crookham, Ewshott and Fleet Cottage Garden and Amateur Show Society was held on Thursday, August 18th at Dinorben Court in a large meadow kindly lent for the occasion ...'. In 1908 Fleet formed its own Horticultural Society— 'This Society was recently formed exclusively for Fleet parish, having disassociated itself from the Crondall, Crookham and Ewshott Horticultural Society'.

During the Second World War scientists from the Royal Aircraft Establishment liaised with a small laboratory, called Power Jets, set up by Frank Whittle, in Leicestershire, which experimented in jet engines. Power Jets had an 'office' in Ively Road next to the National Gas Turbine Establishment and early in the 1950s the whole establishment was brought down to this area, the scientists enhancing the new N.G.T.E. near the Royal Aircraft Establishment. The laboratory was settled on what was known as Pyestock Hill and the families were housed, in council homes especially reserved for them, at both Cove and Church Crookham. The residents of Ryelaw Road, Parsons Close, Johnson Way and other local roads formed a close community of souls torn from home and relocated on a southern boggy heath!

Origins and Landscape

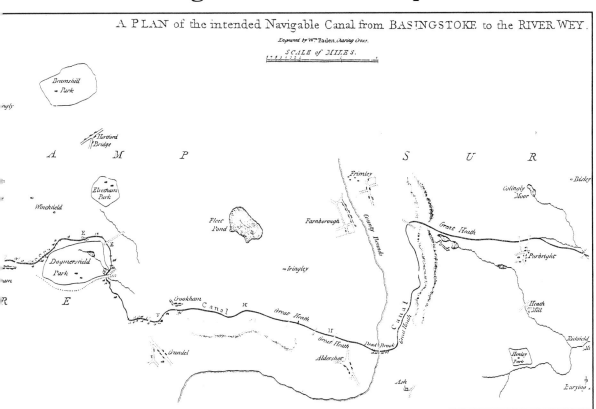

A PLAN of the intended Navigable Canal from BASINGSTOKE to the RIVER WEY.

Engraved by W.ᵐ Faden, charing cross.

SCALE of MILES.

1 Basingstoke Canal, 1777. The intended navigable canal shows an isolated Fleet Pond quite remote from Crookham.

2 Thomas Milne's map of 1791, and the Crondall Hundred, shows Fleet Mill and the Pond divided by a causeway to Bramshot, which subsequently became Cove Road. The position of the canal differs from the route eventually approved and built. Crookham has quite a number of buildings when compared with Farnborough or Aldershot.

13 Market Place, Fleet Road, c.1906. Oakley's Department Store, with its clock tower and cupola, is the landmark by which Fleet became known and continues so today. Opposite Oakley's Store, Darracott's Tea Rooms and Bakery can be seen.

14 Crookham Street, Crookham Village, c.1920. Lavender Cottage, on the right, one half of a 17th-century timber-framed yeoman's home, contains a crude wall painting which has been dated to about 1650. In 1927 the large cedar tree fell across the street demolishing a small wooden barn or shed. The nearby building is still known as Cedar Cottage nearly 70 years later. The corrugated iron social club, opened in 1913, has since been rebuilt and enlarged.

Crookham Street.

15 Crookham Street, *c*.1905. Midway down the street, the view shows two good examples of 17th-century timber-framed cottages with typical half-hipped roofs. On the left Grove and West Views still exist, restored and 'listed' but the building in the middle distance was demolished in the late 1950s. It was known as the 'Pot Shop' probably because it once sold the product of at least two potteries which formerly existed in the village.

16 The swing bridge at Zephon Common in Crookham Village, *c*.1907. There has probably been a swing bridge at this site since the early days of the Basingstoke Canal (opened in 1794): the cast iron balance weights were dated 1840. The bridge shown collapsed when a tank attempted to cross it during the Second World War. It was replaced by an unsatisfactory iron swing footbridge, which in turn has been superseded by the current bridge.

17 Rose Farm Dairy, Fleet Road, shown on the left, was established before 1910 and was close to the then offices of *Fleet News*. The building was later converted to two storeys with main access to the dairy from Albert Street. Rose Farm was one of a number of dairies in Fleet and Crookham at the turn of the century.

18 Frisby's boot and shoe shop in Fleet Road, *c.*1903. By 1910 the business had moved across the road, next door to the Baptist church. Older residents clearly remember a shop lined with orange shoe boxes and assistants in overalls of the same orange shade. The business continued until the 1970s.

19 The post office, Fleet Road, *c*.1904. The site of the second post office, which opened at the turn of the century. Next to the post office was the hairdresser's shop of E. Phillips, who in the same year announced the opening of a second high-class salon in Fleet.

20 Kings Road, Fleet, *c*.1910. This view is from the United Reformed church looking towards Pondtail, showing Akerman's grocery shop on the corner of Clarence Road. Clarence Road, Connaught Road, Albany Road and Kings Road were originally known as Middle Street, High Street, part of Upper Street and Station Road. The renaming was in honour of the Duke of Connaught, who resided in Fleet while G.O.C. of Aldershot Command.

21 Fleet Pond, Fleet, *c.*1906. A tonic for the horse and probably for the cartwheel as well. The view is of the little pond, north of the railway tracks, beside Cove Road, to be partly filled in by the owners of the Country Club in the early 1960s. The water cart was used to lay the dust on the unmade roads.

22 Kimber's Corner, Fleet Road, Fleet, *c.*1903. Looking towards the station from the Kings Road junction with Alfred Pearson's auctioneer and estate agent's business on the corner. The auctions took place, until 1910, in Pinewood Hall to the side of the building shown. On the opposite corner of Kings Road can just be seen Mr. Kimber's off-licence premises.

23 Crookham Road, Fleet, *c*.1916. Originally designated Fleet Road, the location shown is between the police station and the football ground. On the left is the gate leading to Stanton Lodge. The lodge was once part of Boone Farm where Sir Arthur Sullivan was reported to have been a frequent visitor and, it is said, wrote the music for the 'Yeoman of the Guard'.

24 The telephone exchange in Fleet Road, Fleet, *c*.1950. Looking north-eastwards along the Fleet Road from Church Road corner, with the telephone exchange on the left. Built in 1936/7, it was demolished in 1980 and replaced by a new exchange housing an automatic system. The white building in the background was for many years a car showroom and, prior to that, the Gas and Electric showrooms.

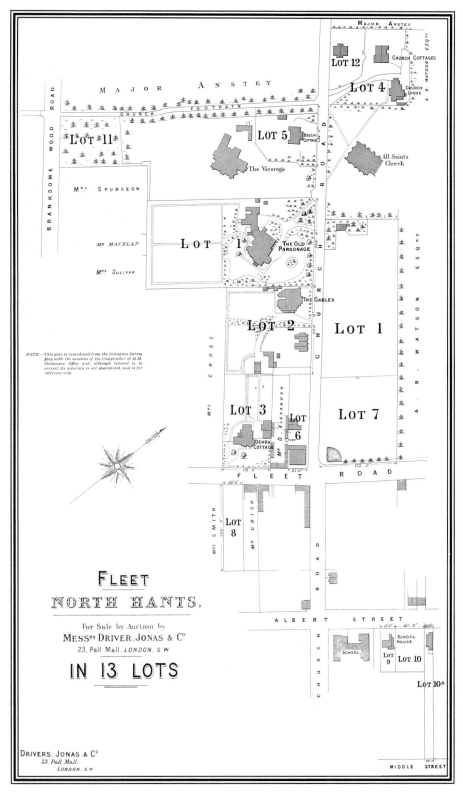

25 This 1908 plan shows the disposition of the variety of lots on offer in the Church Road area of Fleet. It also shows Albert Street School and the Old Parsonage, the site of which contributed a large proportion of the Church Road car park.

26 Connaught Road, Fleet. On a Sunday afternoon today, this is still recognisable as a quiet residential road. Looking towards Kings Road from near Burnside, the 'pavement' trees have matured and gone, but the houses are still there amongst later additions. The pillars on the left are close by today's entrance to Bearwood Gardens. The road was named High Street earlier in the century.

27 Harfield and Fry, Fleet Road, Fleet, *c.*1930. On the left-hand side Harfield and Fry had a toy, sweet and tobacco shop which was demolished in the 1960s. The two or three shops which replaced it were themselves victims of progress in 1989 to make way for one of the entrances to the Hart Centre. Opposite is the porch of Lloyds Bank, formerly the Capital and Counties Bank.

28 Poulter's Bridge, Crookham, 1908, lies between the swing bridge and Chequers Bridge, and is the original structure built over the Basingstoke Canal in 1792. Nearby is Poulters Bridge Cottage, originally a lengthman's cottage, which has been refurbished and enlarged.

29 Reading Road Bridge, *c*.1904. View along the towpath from the waste water weir, looking west. The grounds of 'Heatherside' in Reading Road South come down to the opposite, tree-lined bank.

30 Reading Road Bridge, Fleet, *c*.1906. This photograph shows the second bridge that was erected on this site across the canal. The first bridge was built in 1794, the second in 1898 and a third in 1953. The third bridge was designed to provide a flat road surface by sacrificing headroom over the canal.

31 Avondale Road, Fleet, *c*.1922, showing the Tuck Shop, also a post office, at the corner of Fleet Road and a quiet Avondale Road. The post office business was transferred to nearby Avondale Parade in the 1930s. Some 50 years later, until its demolition, the premises still traded as 'Ye Old Tuckshop'.

Early Developments

32 & 33 Built about 1870, 'The Views' was occupied by Lt. Col. Horniblow from the 1880s to the mid 1930s; possibly he bought it at this sale. He left the grounds of his house—'Views Meadow' which stretched to include Campbell Close— to the people of Fleet. The council took over the house as the new council offices in the late 1930s. The other sale details refer to the 'Gables' at Church Crookham, which was disposed of on the death of the Rev. A. C. Lefroy.

34 Heatherside, Church Crookham, 1907. Built in the 1870s this house remained a private residence in Reading Road South until the 1950s when for a short while it became a hotel. It was subsequently demolished to make way for Heatherside School. Belonging to Heatherside were 'a pair of Capital Cottages for Gardener and Coachman' which still survive today on Reading Road South.

35 The *Prince of Wales*, Church Crookham, *c*.1908. Beyond the *Prince of Wales* on the left was heathland, so there was little need of a pavement. On the right beyond the cottages were the large Court Moor and Basingbourne Estates. Although officially this is Church Crookham, for practical purposes this is an extension of Fleet. George Mansfield was victualler in 1871.

36 *The Oat Sheaf*, Fleet, *c.*1908. Built in the mid-19th century, the public house has changed little over the years. In 1904, Henry Watmore was the proprietor and the hotel offered 'good accommodation for commercial gentlemen, parties, cyclists, etc.'. It boasted nearby cricket, football and hockey grounds.

37 *Fox and Hounds*, Crookham Road, Church Crookham, *c.*1900. Because of its position, the inn has benefited from the Basingstoke Canal and would have seen busy trade from boatmen and the like throughout the 19th century. In more recent years it became a favourite boat hire and mooring point on the canal, particularly on a warm summer evening.

8 Sale of household effects, Fleet, 1904. Pearson's had an established auctioneer's business in Fleet and would have handled most, if not all, such sales. Details show a picture of life at the start of the century with musical tastes, bookbinding and gardening. A governess car was a light, two-wheeled, tub-shaped cart with rear entrance and side seats face to face; the dog cart was of similar size with a compartment for dogs. Broad Street became Wood Lane.

9 *The Fleet Express and District Advertiser* in 1904. In this year the Fleet Urban District Council was established with Col. T. Horniblow as Chairman and Henry Seymour, the Manager of the Capital and Counties Bank, as Treasurer. Inside a full account of the first meeting, held in Fleet Hall, is recorded. A major advertiser was James Oakley and 'The Stores'.

40 Cottage Hospital, Fleet, *c*.1910. The hospital was proposed in 1895 and work commenced in September 1897 on land donated by Lord Calthorpe. The original plan was for a hospital of eight beds in two public wards and one private ward, together with rooms for the Matron and a domestic.

41 Cottage Hospital, Fleet, *c*.1910. The first matron was Miss Ada Strowghill, who was called Nurse-Matron and received £30 per year. She was assisted by one probationer who paid for her own uniform and washing and received no salary. One notable patient was the Duke of Gloucester who was admitted in the 1930s for injuries sustained whilst playing polo in Fleet. At the time, he was stationed in Aldershot with the 4th Hussars.

42 C. & E. Brothers, Fleet Road, *c*.1910. Charles Brothers had taken over the original ironmonger's shop from Mr. H. Blacknell and developed the business together with his brother Edward. The business grew rapidly after the First World War and, because of Charles' son's particular interest, started a department selling battery and mains powered radios, in the inter-war period. Perhaps not surprisingly the site has continued to accommodate building-related activities to the present day. The radio and T.V. business, however, became a separate establishment.

43 Tweseldown racecourse near Church Crookham, *c.*1915. The first steeplechase was held here in 1867 and the Modern Pentathlon competitors in the 1948 Olympics had to negotiate a special course as part of the riding section. A summer camp for Militia (Territorial) units was usually held here; possibly the tents in the distance are from the army camp. The left-hand grandstand was dismantled before the Second World War.

44 *The Wyvern*, Church Crookham, pre-1940. The winged mythical creature with two legs and barbed tail was the emblem of the Lefroy family and it was they who built the inn after the building of Christ Church nearby. In 1885 Thomas Mellersh was publican and grocer at *The Wyvern Arms*, as it was then called. Note the early A.A. sign on the tree.

5 View from Waste Water Bridge, Fleet, *c.*1920. The weir shown was an artificial means of controlling the water level of many miles of the upper half of the Basingstoke Canal, and carried surplus water through Fleet to the Pond. This bridge was situated 100 yards from Reading Road Bridge at a point where the Aldershot Road runs close to the canal.

46 Outside Fleet Station, *c.*1905. A view looking towards Minley Road with Station Approach on the right. The building on the far left is *The Links Hotel* (formerly called the *Station Hotel* and *Fleet Hotel*). The fine row of firs were all eventually removed to make way for road widening.

47 The Broadway, Kings Road, Fleet, *c.*1906. This parade of shops between Albert Street and Clarence Road has not changed substantially since it was built early this century. Vincents, the well-known butchers, ran their business from the corner shop for more than 70 years. A coal merchant with a yard and a second-hand furniture shop occupied other premises for many years.

How Transport Played its Part

48 Cane's Corner, Fleet. A late 19th-century photograph looking towards *The Oat Sheaf* from the Reading Road South corner with Fleet Road, showing the trough being well used by thirsty horses. At this time *The Oat Sheaf* sold Bass & Co. beers. The trough was eventually removed in the late 1960s.

49 Royal Mail being delivered to W. J. Jessett & Sons stores and bakery, Crookham Village, *c*.1908. The main post office for the district was located at Winchfield Station and mail was delivered to sub-offices in the various villages by transport such as that shown here. Crookham mail was distributed from Jessett's stores as well as from Winchfield direct. Mail for Fleet was delivered to Windover's and Dougherty's little stores opposite *The Oat Sheaf*.

50 Steam Roller, Crookham Village, *c*.1900. Such engines were used by local authorities for road repairs and surfacing, relieving many men of their heavy tasks, at a time when early motor cars needed a smoother passage. Traction engines, similar in design except for wheel arrangement, were a common sight on local roads for hauling heavy loads and agricultural equipment. The use of the latter declined in the 1920s and '30s, whilst the steam roller continued to be used until the 1950s for road resurfacing.

51 Fleet Station, *c*.1895. A station was opened at Fleet in 1847 and was known until 1 July 1869 as Fleet Pond Station. It was located on the opposite side of the Minley Road bridge to the station today and there were only two tracks—one up and one down. Remains of the up platform are still visible by the North Hants Golf Club. The station clock still carried the old name for another 70 years.

52 Fleet Station, *c*.1910. Two extra lines were laid, which was the opportunity to transfer the station to its present location. The modern building was opened on 8 March 1904. The photograph shows some-thing of the railways 'customer care' attitude with the covered area, 'porte-cochere', outside the entrance. Fleet was served by steam, and for a short interim period by diesel trains, until 1967 when the line became fully electrified.

53 Hydroplane on Fleet Pond, *c*.1912. Geoffrey de Havilland experimented with an aeroplane of his own design and construction as early as 1908. He was possibly the pilot of this Farnborough-built biplane taking off and landing on Fleet Pond. In his log-book he recorded numerous flights using biplane designs from April 1912. B.E.2 was the factory's most famous aeroplane. He was often accompanied by P. M. Green, Chief Engineer at Farnborough.

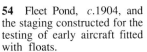

54 Fleet Pond, *c*.1904, and the staging constructed for the testing of early aircraft fitted with floats.

55 An iceboat on Fleet Pond in the winter of 1929. This looks like a motorised float from an aeroplane, fitted with skids, being used to produce an ingenious ice float on the frozen Fleet Pond.

56 A Fleet Volunteer Fire Brigade vehicle, *c.*1920. Great progress was being made in the 1920s when the horse-drawn fire tender was replaced with the new motor-driven version, shown here outside the council offices next to the fire station in Albert Street. The council, guardian of rate-payers' money, would have preferred to supply a faster horse to replace 'Sam'—but were under pressure to move into the modern age!

57 Ivy Laundry, Church Crookham, *c.*1920. The delivery fleet is outside the Aldershot premises with smart drivers in uniform. Each vehicle shows different white flasher design and coachwork advertising. A booklet, from which this photograph was taken, states the directors as G. C. and H. M. Carpenter and notes 1895 as the date the laundry was established.

58 Fleet Coaches, *c*.1940
On 22 March 1934 William
Davies and his son William
George Davies, registered the
business in 7 Crookham Road
then known as Fleet Road, as
a motor repair workshop. In
1948 William George, the
son, and his wife Queenie
bought their first coach, a 20
seater, and painted it cream
and black. Davies Coaches
had been born. Later the name
was changed to Fleet Coaches
and the livery to the now well
known two-tone blue.

59 The showrooms of
Stevens & Sons, Fleet, *c*.1925
and a selection of hand
operated milk floats made in
the carpentry shop.

STEVENS & SONS, FLEET, HANTS.

60 Stevens Bros., Fleet, *c.*1955. Mr. Stevens, a Crookham smith, opened a second smithy and coach building business in Fleet Road. The premises extended through to Albert Street. His six sons were each apprenticed to a different but relevant trade and the business logically progressed to 'horseless carriages'. It became a thriving car sale and repair business and petrol pumps were added. The business closed in the late 1960s.

61 Fleet Station, 1955. St Nicholas School boarders waiting on Fleet Station platform prior to departing for home at the end of the summer term. Notice the porter's trolley and covered pedestrian bridge.

62 A charabanc outing from Fleet to Southsea, *c.*1927. The vehicle owner and driver was Mr. Lukey who lived in Fleet Road. The photograph was taken at Southsea.

63 Crompton Tapp's three roller motor roller, *c.*1910. Ernest Tapp (on the left) was the inventive one of the two brothers who formed County Commercial Cars in 1929.

64 A 'Surrey', County Commercial Cars, Fleet. This design, by Ernest Tapp, of a six-wheeler design, termed a 'Surrey', was originally built for the brothers' transport company. The truck formed the basis of the creation of County Commercial Cars. The name 'County Commercial Cars' originated from trucks being commonly called commercial cars and the models were named after the English counties.

65 A 'Sussex', County Commercial Cars, Fleet. By the mid-1930s the business was well established in the old council offices in Albert Street. The Sussex chassis with double-drive axle was chosen by the Air Ministry and War Office to be the standard six-wheeled transport for the Second World War. It was a proud boast at County that there was a Sussex at the other end of the cable on all land-based barrage balloons.

66 'Devon Tug', County Commercial Cars, Fleet. This was another version of the three wheeler called the Devon Tug. The earlier Devon Van was produced before the Second World War by Ford Motor Company. The Devon Tug had its own automatic coupling for the trailer.

67 Crawler Tractor, County Commercial Cars, Fleet. County decided to produce a crawler tractor. The initial model produced was of narrow gauge, for pest control, but it was clear there was a market for a normal gauge crawler and the County agricultural crawler was born. It became the leading tractor of this type produced in the U.K., the early prototypes were based on the Fordson Tractor.

68 Super 4s, County Commercial Cars, Fleet. Two Super 4s in front of the County office in Albert Street, which was demolished to accommodate the Hart Shopping Centre. These became probably the most successful four-wheel drive tractors in the world, being sold to over 200 countries. Production at its peak reached 40 units per week for the Super 4 and its derivatives. They were a common sight along the Fleet Road on their way to the station.

The Rôle of the Church

William Webster, b.1798, d.1887. The *Fleet Monthly Reporter* obituary of 22 January 1887 observed that . Webster could be considered the pioneer of all ristian work at Fleet, having founded Hope Chapel. He ided in the locality for some 30 years; in the beginning re was no church nor chapel and scarcely any houses. established a successful boys' boarding school and residence and school still exist as a private house.

Crookham Church

70 Christ Church, Crookham, was established in 1840. The initiative to build a church for the new parish came chiefly from Charles Edward Lefroy. He was a friend of John Keble, a leading member of the Oxford Movement. Land was acquired on Gally Hill and a fund was started to erect an ecclesiastical building large enough to seat 400 people. The first stone was laid in March 1840 and Christ Church was dedicated by Henry Sumner, Bishop of Winchester, in 1841. Anthony Conttrell Leyfroy, Charles' nephew, became the first incumbent. The church was designed by Woodyer in the Early English style.

71 Sgraffito, Christ Church, Crookham. The decorations on the chancel walls are termed sgraffiti. They date from 1893 and were designed and executed by Heywood Sumner, a leading figure in the Arts and Crafts Movement and a grandson of the Bishop of Winchester. The sgraffito process is laborious, depending upon successive layers of plaster, plain and coloured, which harden and are then cut to reveal the required design.

72 & 73 Ebenezer Baptist Chapel, Fleet, *c.*1890. Built in 1859, this chapel in Reading Road North, a few yards from *The Oat Sheaf*, was in use for a number of years until a new chapel was built nearby which opened in 1892. The chapel was converted in the 1950s into a garage for the adjoining house and was eventually demolished to make way for commercial office development.

74 All Saints' parish church, Fleet, *c.*1905. All Saints', consecrated in 1862, has great architectural merit, being the work of one of the leading architects of the day, William Burges. The need for a church in a growing Fleet in the mid-19th century was recognised by Charles Edward Lefroy. He also saw this new church as a memorial to his wife.

75 Interior of All Saints' Church, Fleet, pre-1934. Burges was an exponent of the English Gothic Revival. The interior was visually impressive—bare red brick with appliqué designs decorating the chancel and apse. In 1949 some of the designs were obliterated with whitewash from lack of appreciation of the 19th-century decoration. The founder and his wife lie on the table tomb on the left. This also bears the family arms which include two red wyverns.

76 The Rev. Wilfred Gordon Wickham was the first pastor at Christ Church to hold the title 'Vicar', bestowed in 1890. Known affectionately as Parson Bill, he was vicar from 1883-1925 having succeeded his brother Gordon Boles Wickham (1875-1883).

77 Mission Room, Crookham Village. The corrugated iron 'Mission Room' on the right of Crookham Street was built in 1891 as a Chapel of Ease for elderly residents, for whom Christ Church, Church Crookham was a long walk one and a half miles away. It continued in occasional use for early services and Sunday School until 1972, when it was demolished.

78 Wesleyan Church, Branksomewood Road, Fleet, *c*.1900. The first wooden Wesleyan Methodist Church was erected in 1887 on a site at the junction of Branksomewood Road and Fleet Road. In 1899 it had become too small, and a large brick and stone church, shown here, was built on the same site facing Fleet Road. It was demolished in the late 1960s when a new Methodist church was built in Reading Road South.

79 New Primitive Methodist Church, Church Crookham, 1880s. This church was built in 1883 in Reading Road South, and a schoolroom was added in 1898. The two Methodist churches united in 1963 and by 1966 all services were held at Reading Road South. A site adjacent to the church was purchased and the present Methodist Church was opened in 1972.

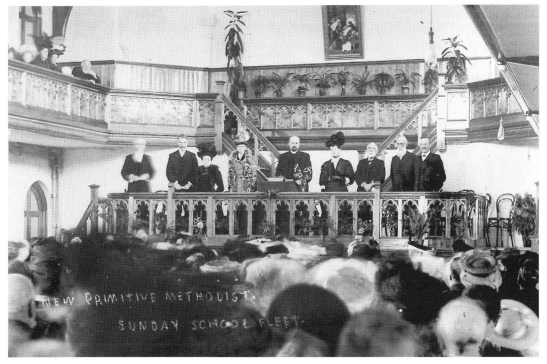

80   Wesleyan Sunday Schools, Fleet, *c*.1912. This handsome Assembly Room (the school room is on the left) was the work of Stanley Pool (architect) and stood together with the Wesleyan Church on the corner of Branksomewood Road and Fleet Road. When the two Methodist churches in Fleet combined (the other was in Reading Road South) this site was sold and is now occupied by a large store.

81   In 1850, those who died as Dissenters attending Hope Chapel were refused burial by local clergy and this led to the opening of the chapel burying ground. This memorial card records the burial of Ruth Lawrence in Hope Chapel cemetery. Though the chapel has gone, the cemetery still exists off Reading Road North, next to the site of William Webster's original chapel and boys' boarding school.

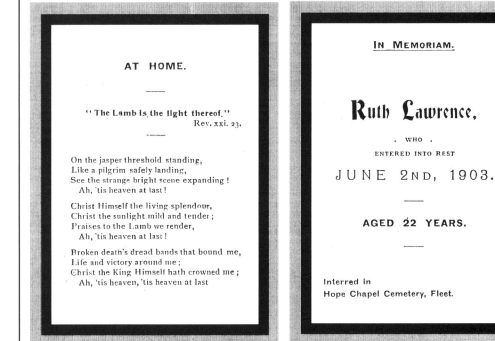

82 The Crossways in Crookham Village, *c*.1905. A very full band of the Salvation Army, probably from Fleet, two miles distant, accompanying a typical open-air service on a rather chilly May morning. The band almost outnumber the congregation. This picture was taken by the late George Jessett from the balcony of his shop.

83   The United Reformed Church in Fleet was founded in 1912. By 1913 finances were available to build a church for Congregational worshippers. Up to this time services had been held in the Pinewood Hall, Fleet Road. The church was officially opened in July 1914 and, much later in 1964, the Sunday School Hall was built. In 1972 the Congregational Church and Presbyterian Church united and the church became a member of the United Reformed Church.

84   Fleet Baptist Chapel, *c.*1930. In 1893 this building, located at the Oatsheaf crossroads, replaced the Hope Chapel which was situated near the Baptist cemetery. This site was satisfactory until the road widening scheme in the late 1960s disturbed the peace too much, when a new site was found in Clarence Road. Demolition took place in the 1970s when a parade of shops was built.

The Military Connection

85 & 86 Tweseldown camp later Haig Lines, *c.*1914. Haig Lines, or Hutments, were built and established at Church Crookham and initially housed an Officer Cadet Training Battalion. From about 1920 this camp became the Depot and Training Establishment for the Royal Army Medical Corps (R.A.M.C.). From 1939 it was used as a reception centre both for reservists called to the colours and throughout the Second World War for the Canadian Army. After the war the camp became the base for mechanised cavalry units. The Duke of Kent served here with the Royal Scots Greys. During the Hungarian uprising of 1956 the huts were used as a transit camp for refugees. The huts were demolished in the 1980s to make way for residential housing.

View of Lines from Aldershot Road.

87 Haig Lines, Church Crookham, *c.*1920. As this was an R.A.M.C. camp, men from other units would probably attend first aid courses here. Any member of the Corps serving throughout the world would be very familiar with this scene.

88 Haig Lines, *c.*1925. This photograph shows an interior view with the trestle tables laid out in one of the men's dining halls. A similar photograph for the sergeants' dining halls indicates much less spartan surroundings. Such cards were sent back home to reassure the family.

One of the Men's Dining Halls.

89 Ewshot Camp, near Church Crookham, *c*.1914. The Leipzig Barracks for the R.F.A. were originally built at Ewshot in 1900, and the Punjab and Quetta Quarters were added later. This photograph shows soldiers on parade at Ewshot Camp. The area is now Quetta Park Military Married Quarters.

90 Refreshment time, Tweseldown summer camp, *c*.1914. Richard Pool had a removals business in Fleet and Hartley Wintney and was called upon to assist Army Units in the vicinity. Here a vehicle is being used for catering in the field. Note among the group several officer cadets (white cap bands) from miscellaneous regiments.

91 R.F.A., Crookham Village, *c.*1914. Brigade of the R.F.A. in column passing westward through Crookham Street. Although fully equipped, there is no sign of steel helmets which were introduced in 1916. This unit would almost certainly be from Leipzig Barracks, Ewshot, a permanent home for the R.F.A. since 1901. The very new corrugated iron Social Club was built in 1913.

92 Temporary War Memorial, Fleet, 1919. Peace celebrations took place in the summer of 1919. As there was then no permanent War Memorial, a temporary one was erected in Fleet Road, opposite the post office, on land forming part of Pool & Sons sawmill site.

93 War Memorial, Fleet, 1921. The memorial, built by local stonemasons Mardles, was sited close by Fleet Road on land donated by the *Station Hotel*. The scene shows the unveiling ceremony on Sunday, 10 April 1921. The white Portland Stone memorial was removed to the Library precinct in the 1970s because of traffic congestion which occurred each Armistice Day at the original site. It was moved again when the new council offices were built in 1985.

94 First Aid parties, Fleet, 1943/4, assembled in front of their vehicles. The photograph was taken at The Views, Fleet. Col. A. F. S. Fennel, shown in the middle of the front row, was the Civil Defence Officer/Controller. The drummer, Frank Hoar, kept them all in step on drill parades and processions.

95 Civil Defence, tug-of-war team, 1944. A winning tug-of-war team! Civil Defence was originally known as Air Raid Precautions. Recruitment commenced in 1937/38 when the threat of war was growing. This team won the Aldershot Borough Cup, Lilywhite Challenge Cup, Horticultural Society Cup and 'Under 20' Cup.

96 A V.E. day street party in 1945. Parties such as this one in Clarence Road, Fleet, were taking place throughout the country. Trestle tables were set up in the street to give the local children a tea party, generally followed by races and games. Sometimes each child was given a certificate to say he or she attended.

97 V.E. day celebrations at Crookham School, 1945.

98 The visit on 23 June 1948 of Queen Elizabeth (now the Queen Mother), Colonel-in-Chief to the Corps Training Establishment, Church Crookham, on the occasion of the R.A.M.C. Golden Jubilee (1898-1948). Redfields House, from about 1940 until the corps moved, provided an excellent Officers' Mess.

99 Gurkha Museum, Church Crookham. Gurkha regiment have been stationed at Queen Elizabeth Barracks in Sand Lane since 1971. These cheerful soldiers from Nepal have been very popular in Fleet and Crookham, particularly on their parades to and from overseas duties. A museum of their history in the British Army was sited at the barracks until recently, when it was transferred to Peninsular Barracks, Winchester.

100 Sergeant Thomas Mitten, M.S.M., lived in Rochester Grove and was a familiar figure in Fleet from the '20s until he died. On special occasions he wore his pre-1914 scarlet with cloth of gold sergeant's stripes and crimson sash, medals and blue and gold spiked helmet. In 1944 he was presented to Princess Elizabeth (now Queen Elizabeth II) and in the same year he was awarded the Meritorious Service Medal, with an annuity of £10, largely in recognition of his efforts for charity.

At Work ...

01 The forge and forge house, Crookham Village, *c*.1905. The house was built in the early or mid-17th century, whilst the forge shown is probably mid-19th-century. The ring of hammer on anvil could be heard in the village street until the 1950s. The Stevens family operated the business for over a century and moved to the rapidly expanding town of Fleet in the 1890s.

102 Post office staff, Fleet, *c*.1906. The staff of the post office soon after it opened in 1906. The doors finally closed in 1990.

103 Postmen at the post office, Fleet, *c*.1910. An informal photograph of postmen at the end of their shift (the caps denote those who are off-duty). The postman at the extreme left wearing leggings and a helmet was in charge. He had a crown on his lapels denoting a Postman Higher Grade.

104 Hop picking, Crookham Village, *c.*1910. The H.W. on the bin refers to Harry White of Grove Farm, and the pickers are known to be locals, mostly from cottages beside the Basingstoke Canal. At least three farms had extensive hop gardens until the 1930s, whilst Grove Farm continued production until 1974 when the lack of local pickers and the increasing popularity of lager, for which the local hop was unsuitable, led to the end of hop growing in Crookham.

105 Ivy Laundry, Church Crookham, *c*.1910. This laundry in Grove Road, near Crookham crossroads, was founded in 1895 by G. C. and H. M. Carpenter, but by 1905 it was in the hands of C. Crane. In 1910 the premises opposite were occupied by the Royal Standard Laundry. Both laundries had closed by 1929. The ironing room was situated in the building on the left.

106 Ivy Laundry, *c*.1910. The ironing room demonstrates concern for safety—electric cables were overhead and not trailing on the floor. There was some ventilation and plenty of natural light. However, one can feel the steamy heat, the tired backs and feet, and hear the chatter in such a crowded workplace as this.

All Ex-Service Men should Join the

British Legion

Apply to the Secs.:
Mr. R. H. POWELL and
Mr. L. EDMONDS.

Fleet & Crookham
CHAMBER OF COMMERCE
Journal

Shop Locally

and keep the

Bus Fares

in your pocket.

No. 2   MAY, 1924   Gratis

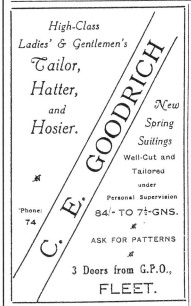

Current Topics
of
Local Interest.

"Fleet, Hants."

Protests against the new postal address—"Fleet, Aldershot"—continue to be made to the Postal Authorities. The Urban District Council protested strongly when the change was first suggested, and has just recently endorsed the protest of the local Ratepayers' Association. At the last meeting of the Council on May 8th, the Post Master at Aldershot informed the Council that the resolution was being considered. While the matter is still *sub judice*, further comment need not be made, except that it is a change upon which many residents feel sore.

Bringing Home the Cup.

Fleet Football Club are to be highly congratulated on bringing home the Camberley Hospital Cup. An achievement such as this not only serves as a stimulus to the players themselves, but increases interest in the Club by the public generally, and incidentally adds to the prestige of the place which the Postal Authorities are anxious to dub as "Fleet Aldershot," but which residents prefer to retain as "Fleet, Hants."

The Fleet team had a unique struggle to get in the final, which they only reached after an extraordinary run of extra-time play, and the players well earned the medals which fell to their lot. The Charity for which the Cup is promoted should benefit considerably by the re-plays, and particularly by the final at Camberley, when it appeared that nearly all Fleet were present to encourage the local team. Fleet evidently seemed to be the favourite team of the day, one youth being heard to remark that he had "come all the way from Frimley to see Fleet win the Cup."

Goosey-Goosey-Gander.

The pet goose—or it may be a gander!—belonging to a well known tradesman, is fast becoming a favourite. Its quaint antics in the street simply delight the hearts of the children, and prove quite amusing to many an adult. The bird as befits one of such enviable distinction, is evidently a little particular with whom it associates. If it does not wish to reciprocate the kind remarks of a passer-by, it does not hesitate to say so, with extended neck and spread-eagled wings, in the orthodox goosey way.

This now famous bird takes quite a knowing interest in local affairs, whether it be road making, hedge trimming, or what sometimes

Continued on Page 8.

---

107   *Fleet and Crookham Chamber of Commerce* journal, 1924. This is a re-issue of the journal which had previously fallen on hard times—the editor, in issue 1, argued the case for more advertising. The Chamber of Commerce Chairman's comments, inside the journal, were printed under the same badge depicting pine trees as illustrated in picture no. 8.

108 Tobacco workers at Redfields, Church Crookham, c.1920, are shown here preparing leaves for drying. Mr. A. J. Brandon bought Redfields House and estate and began to grow tobacco there in 1911. At its peak in the 1920s he utilised 18 acres and produced various types of tobacco, almost exclusively for cigarette manufacturing by H. Stevens & Co. of Salisbury. Mr. Brandon fought hard to persuade the Government to repeal the Imperial Preference Tax which favoured Commonwealth products.

109 A tobacco worker at Redfields, Church Crookham, c.1920. Mr. Brandon was reported to be the main English grower and he established a reputation for his campaign for home grown tobacco. Redfields produced a variety of brands—the best known was Blue Pryor—others were Smyrna, Samos, Burley and Green Dragon.

110 Tobacco workers at Redfields, *c*.1920. The end of major production came in 1937 with Mr. Brandon's death. An unsuccessful attempt was made to re-establish the industry in later years. Redfields became a conference/training centre, whilst the last remaining evidence of tobacco making, the drying sheds, were demolished in the 1970s. The bewhiskered gentleman, Mr. Smith, was the foreman. Most, if not all, of the workers were local villagers.

111 Saunders Nurserie
Fleet, 1956. The 'Albert Stre
Nurseries' were opened by '
Ayres in the early years o
this century and eventuall
glasshouses were built ne:
to the family home in Fle
Road, almost opposite Birc
Avenue. In 1923, Mr. A
Saunders bought the premis
and stayed there until h
retired in 1966, when the
demolished.

112 Crumplin's, Readir
Road South, Fleet, *c*.193
Crumplin's Hairdresser's sho
opened in 1925 in Readir
Road South, near the Fle
Road junction. Alf Crumpl:
(right) and Fred Godde
subsequently transferred '
premises on the opposite si
of Reading Road; the busine
closed in the 1960s. Like Al
Fred Godden carried o
cycling around Fleet to c
hair in the comfort o
customers' homes.

113 Crookham Volunteer Fire Brigade, 1925. The brigade was justly proud of trophies for efficiency and smartness, as apparent in the photograph. Doubtless this was to the credit of their Captain, ex-Cavalry Sergeant Major Frederick Liming. The driver and his mate were the Dockerill Brothers, garage proprietors, who were retained as engineers. The gentleman on the right hand side is George Knight, secretary and ex-vice captain.

114 Remains of a narrow boat, Chequers Bridge, *c.*1930. The winding hole on the Basingstoke Canal at Crookham Village. The bridge takes its name from the *Chequers* pub nearby. Canal Cottage in the background was once the base for the local lengthmen and bailiff and is believed to have been the office of the original company which advertised the opening of the canal in 1794. The narrow boat *Tipton* was last used to carry oak and her remains lay here for over 60 years until they were removed in the late 1980s.

115 Pool's sawmill, Fleet, *c.*1916. Herbert Pool developed a home grown timber-mill business from 1914-49. The sawmill established in Fleet Road, stretching to Albert Street, was a temporary provision for wartime. Timber was felled and drawn from the nearby Elvetham estate lands, and power was provided by steam engines which burnt waste wood.

116 Invoice from Pool & Sons, Fleet, *c.*1908. At this early date, in their original location at the rear of the Baptist Church near the Oatsheaf crossroads, the firm clearly planned to build up a builder's merchants' business, but it seems never to have developed.

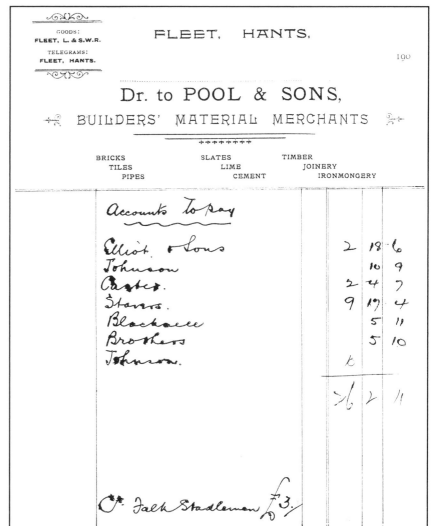

GOODS:
FLEET, L. & S.W.R.
TELEGRAMS:
FLEET, HANTS.

FLEET, HANTS.

Dr. to POOL & SONS,
BUILDERS' MATERIAL MERCHANTS

BRICKS   SLATES   TIMBER
TILES   LIME   JOINERY
PIPES   CEMENT   IRONMONGERY

Accounts To pay			
Elliot & Sons	2	18	6
Johnson		10	9
Castle.	2	4	7
Starrs.	9	17	4
Blackall		5	11
Brothers		5	10
Johnson.		£	
	2/6	2	11

Cr. Jack Stadleman £3.

117 Gally Hill brick, *c.*1900. Earliest references state that in 1880 H. Woolf Cohen of 18-19 High Street, Aldershot had a brick works at Gally Hill, Crookham. The claypit is now an ornamental lake in the garden at the Grange Estate of Gally Hill Road. In 1885, the proprietors were Messrs. Parks and Marshall—The P. & M. denoted on the brick. Another brickyard, Crookham Brick & Tile Company, operated until 1908 from a site at Zephon Common, near the Basingstoke Canal.

18 Jessett & Sons, Crookham Village, 1920s. Mr. William Jessett (centre) with his staff outside the stables. Mr. Albert Tiller is third from left. Mr. Jessett donned a baker's hat and shop apron for the photograph. Besides running the grocery and bakery departments, he was more usually seen at the post office desk. His brother, George, the official postmaster and a good amateur photographer, ran the clothing and drapery department.

19 Jessett's Stores and Bakery, Crookham Village. Delivery vans and traps served customers well beyond Crookham Village itself: Church Crookham, Pilcot, Dogmersfield, Winchfield and Fleet were included. Residents today remember the store, which was at the junction of Crondall and Pilcot Roads, with affection.

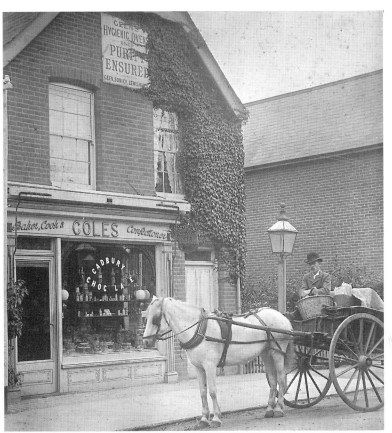

120 Coles Bakery, Fleet. The picture was taken in the 1920s and shows the delivery cart and driver in front of the premises in Fleet Road. The sign outside proclaims that teas and coffee could be consumed on the premises. The shop in the mid-1920s became Weavers, then in the late 1930s Allen the bakers. Before the bakery's closure, many items were removed to the Old Kiln Museum, Tilford.

121 The Art Laundry, Fleet, 1935. This brochure shows the premises decorated for the 1935 Silver Jubilee celebrations. The Art Laundry was on the corner of Kenilworth and Avondale Roads. After the war Dae Health Laboratories took over the premises for their packing operation. The building was demolished in the 1960s.

... And At Play

122 In 1896, T. H. Smelt ran a photographic studio at Cyprus House, Victoria Road, and advertised that he had 'distinguished' patronage. The men in the group are in the ceremonial dress of the Ancient Order of Foresters, which that year had 70 members. The order was established in Fleet in 1884 and held its meetings in the Albert Street School Rooms.

THE QUEEN'S
DIAMOND JUBILEE
COMMEMORATION.

CROOKHAM, JULY 29, 1897

ORDER OF PROCEEDINGS.

12.30 Procession Starts from Crookham Street (headed by Fleet Brass Band).

1. 0 Meeting of Parishioners at the School.

1.30 Dinner in the Grounds of Crookham House.

3. 0 Tea for Children.

3.30 Sports. See Programme.

4.30 Winding the Maypole.

7. 0 Presentation of Prizes.

9.30 Parade of Cyclists in Costume.
Meet at School at 9 p.m.
Three Prizes will be given to the best turn-out.

After which there will be

A Grand Display of Sixty Rockets,
Commemorating the years of Her Majesty's Long Reign.

Refreshments will be served at Moderate Prices during the Afternoon and Evening.

Tea (First-class) 2d. per cup.   Cake, &c, 1d. per slice.
  „ (Second-class) 1d. per cup.   Ditto.

Matthews' Roundabouts will be in Attendance.
Grounds will be Closed at 11 p.m.

PROGRAMME OF SPORTS.

Best Decorated Bicycle. Three prizes

Tug of War (men) Married v. Married, 8 each side 12/-

Tug of War (men) Single v. Single, 8 each side 12/-

Tug of War (women) Married v. Married, 12 each side

Tug of War (women) Single v. Single, 12 each side

200 Yards (men) under 25. Three prizes

200 Yards (men) over 25. Three prizes

Three-legged Race (boys) under 15. Two prizes

High Jump. Two prizes.

Stone Race (boys) under 15. Three prizes

Stone Race (girls) under 15. Three prizes

Wheelbarrow Race, boys under 15. Two prizes

Wheelbarrow Race, males over 15. Two prizes

100 Yards, women (married). Two prizes

100 Yards, women (single). Two prizes

Slow Bicycle Race, 100 yards. Two Prizes

Sack Race. Three prizes

100 Yards (boys) under 15. Three prizes

100 Yards (girls) under 15. Three prizes

Veterans' Race, 100 yards, Men over 50. Two prizes

Quarter-mile Handicap. Two Prizes

Good prizes commemorating the Queen's Diamond Jubilee will be given in each event.

It is particularly requested that all names for the various events should be given to Rev. W. G. Wickham, not later than Tuesday, July 27th.

Four entries for each event or no race.

123 A Diamond Jubilee Commemoration leaflet of 1897. When the whole neighbourhood was brought together in 1897 everyone 'knew their place ... 1st Class and 2nd Class teas'. A long day, by all accounts, and one can almost hear the steam engine working Matthew's roundabouts. One hopes the vicar had a good team of helpers.

124 The Fleet & District Fanciers' Association was formed in 1904 to 'foster interest in the rearing of fancy and utility poultry in the district'. Later it expanded its interests to include rabbits, cage birds and cats. The two-day show was held in the New Hall and this 1908 prize card was for Class 79!

FLEET & DISTRICT FANCIERS' ASSOCIATION.

OPEN SHOW,   Aug. 19 & 20, 1908.

THIRD PRIZE.

Awarded to _____

Class _____   Pen _____

President :
J. LINDSAY JOHNSTON, Esq., J.P., C.C.

J. OAKLEY, Esq.,   F. T. L. AVIS & F. HESTER,
Chairman and Treasurer.   Hon. Secs.

Copyright.   Drew, Show Printer, Aldershot.

125 The North Hants Golf Club, Minley Road, Fleet, *c.*1910. This exclusive golf club was opened on 6 May 1904 by Princess Alice of Teck. Originally a private residence known as the Beeches, it was owned by Mr. Bloore, a London timber merchant. A croquet lawn and tennis courts were sited on what is now the practice area. Note the decorative bargeboard.

126 A brochure from the late 1950s showing the North Hants club house before the laying out of a large patio across the front and the building of an extension on the right.

127 A boating regatta on Basingstoke Canal, 1919. Boating was a regular pastime on the canal and this peace celebration regatta was well attended by officer cadets on the bank opposite the towpath. Mr. H. Cox hired boats from his shed near Reading Road Bridge.

128 The Garth Hunt at Crookham Village, *c.*1920. Local house sale details of 1910 stated that 'hunting can be enjoyed with Mr. Garth's foxhounds two or three days a week'. Between 1926 and 1928 the Masters of the Hunt were Lt. Col. Lord Dorchester of Greywell Hill and Mr. Herbert S. Chinnock of Dinorben Court, Fleet. In 1950, the Hunt became known as the Garth and South Berks.

129 A feature of Crookham life at Christmas is the performance by the Mummers, seen here in 1932, enacting a play whose origins are obscure but which has been seen in the locality for over 100 years. Weirdly dressed characters represent the Turkish Knight, Father Christmas, King George, Bold Roamer, Bold Slasher, Johnny Jack (also known as Trim Tram) and the Doctor.

130 Fleet Football team, 1923. The photograph was taken to celebrate the opening on 3 March of the club's new ground off Crookham Road. Those shown include Steve Sayers, Pecky Vass,—Slingo,—Lunn, Fred Eggleton, Len Edwards and Frank Hoar (trainer). In 1929, they were photographed in a different strip as winners of the Frere Cup.

131 The Fleet Scout Group, *c.*1920. The troop is shown outside the New Hall in Fleet Road near the site of the first telephone exchange. The soldier appears to be wearing the badge of the R.A.M.C. Local scouting was perhaps a little more military orientated than usual, due to the wealth of available service instructors and retired officers.

132 Cinema programme, *c.*1930. The Fleet Hall, built in 1891 in Fleet Road, was said to be able to seat 500 people. It became the Bioscope, Paladium, then King George's Cinema, and later the County, one of a local circuit. In 1937 the circuit owner, Mr. Donada, sold out to Odeon (its final name) who were expanding nationally, and the renovated cinema was formally opened by Florence Desmond. By the mid-1950s television was becoming more popular and Fleet's only public cinema closed.

Monday, December 1st, for three days :

MARY EATON, in
Glorifying the Show Girl
A masterpiece of revue and romance. Captivating song hits, lavish settings, wonderful choruses, scintillating colour scenes and a gripping story.

Thursday, December 4th, for three days :

IN THE HEADLINES
With Grant Withers & Marian Nixon.
All-Talking. A pretty girl—a young reporter—a murder ! Romance and mystery, with the seething activity of newspaper offices.

TALKING COMEDY, "Her Hired Husband."

Sunday, December 7th :

Charles Rogers and Nancy Carroll
in
ILLUSION
The "Close Harmony" Stars in an All-Talking reality.

Monday, December 8th, for Six Days :
The Sensational All-Colour, Talking-Singing-Dancing Success !

GOLD-DIGGERS OF BROADWAY
Featuring CONWAY TEARLE, ANN PENNINGTON, WINNIE LIGHTNER and a brilliant cast. Without doubt the jolliest and most tuneful film that has been produced. Simply crammed with songs, humour, gorgeous scenes and beautiful girls.

Sunday, December 14th :
Special Fleet & Crookham Fire Brigades Night
PROGRAMME TO BE ANNOUNCED LATER.

Monday, December 15th, for three days :

SEYMOUR HICKS,
in
SLEEPING PARTNERS
With EDNA BEST and LYN HARDING The first appearance of Seymour Hicks on the Talking Screen. A delightful farce from Sacha Guitry's successful stage play.

TALKING COMEDY : "All-Stuck Up."

Thursday, December 18th, for three days :
CHARLES "BUDDY" ROGERS
With JEAN ARTHUR, in

HALF-WAY TO HEAVEN
All-Talking. Love and jealousy in the circus. See the devilish revenge the trapeze artist prepares for his rival. Danger and Daring ! Risks and Romance !

TALKING COMEDY : "Pick 'Em Young."

Sunday, December 21st :
CORINNE GRIFFITH, in
The Divine Lady
with H. B. WARNER and VICTOR VARCONI.

Monday, December 22nd, for three days :
William Powell and Helen Kane, in
POINTED HEELS
All-Talking. Girls and music. Songs and fun ! A most entertaining production with a brilliant revue in natural colours

Also :
HAROLD LLOYD in "Why Worry"
A revival of that famous silent Comedy.

133 Fleet Town Prize Brass Band, *c*.1934. The band shown outside the band hall in Clarence Road. The players are: *back row*: Bunting, Loveday, Dunford, Fordell, Lunn, Berry; *middle row*: Soane, Coppard, Eales, Oram, Smith, Sayers, Barker, Chapman; *front row*: Chapman, Loveday, Tocock, Hill, Hyson, Corp, Hoar.

134 Fleet Silver Band, *c*.1930. The bands (see 133) were rivals until after the war when they merged. This merger proved unsuccessful and the players disbanded around 1947. Band members included: Mills, Hoar, Woolley, Gordner, Johnson, Robinson, Mills (jnr.), W. Woolley, C. Robinson, Wooldridge, Burton and Wallace.

135 The Forest Hut near the Basingstoke Canal, *c*.1930. Before the Second World War there was a wooden building near Norris Bridge which served teas at weekends. It was reached by a pleasant row on the canal from either the Fleet or Aldershot boathouses.

136 & 137 In 1931 there were two full polo grounds and a practice ground at Ancells Farm in Cove Road, Fleet. Sale details in 1925 refer to Wellington Polo Club one mile distant from Elvetham Road, and this could have been the original name. Fleet played in white and the season ran from May to September. The photographs show all that remained of the pavilion and changing room at the Fleet Polo Club, Ancells Farm, before their demolition. The club was affiliated to the Hurlingham Polo Association in the 1930s and fielded a number of teams.

138 The Girls Friendly Society's tableau assembled in Albany Road. It was awarded second prize in the 1936 Fleet Hospital Carnival. On board were Bertha Hoar, Joan Tapsell, Lizzie Knowles, Joan O'Hara, Agnes Standen, Olive Lunn, Ellen Askell, Joyce Terry, Phyllis Slingo, Bernie Eales, Violet Askell, Jean Lunn, Hazel Higgins and Mr. Salter.

139 Fleet Carnival, 1957. Always attracting large and appreciative crowds along the route, the carnival progresses along Fleet Road with the Farnborough St John Ambulance Pipe Band in the lead. The Carnival Queen tableau was drawn by a County Commercial tractor.

140 Silver Jubilee celebrations, Fleet, 1935. This is possibly a typical example of the celebration of King George V and Queen Mary's 25-year reign seen anywhere in Britain and the Empire. The names of Sigmund Romberg, Sidney Dacre and Henry Hall are still remembered, but what of those who assisted the band?

SILVER JUBILEE CELEBRATIONS, FLEET. MAY, 1935. # OLD PEOPLE'S TEA (Arranged by Mr. W. H. Hepper) AT THE NEW HALL FOLLOWED BY AN ENTERTAINMENT By FLEET PRIZE BRASS BAND (Under the direction of Mr. Jas. A. Hill) ASSISTED BY Mrs. BIRCHAM, Mrs. SHEENA GUISE, Mr. W. CARDEN, Mr. J. G. WILCOX. PIANIST : Miss D. THOMPSON.	# PROGRAMME. March ... "Our Noble King" ... ... E. Newton Fantasia ... ... "Dawn of Spring" ... E. Le Duc Song ... ... Selected ... Mrs. BIRCHAM Selection ... ... "Desert Song" ... ... Romberg Song ... ..." Any Dirty Work To-day " W. CARDEN Selection ... "Day in Coon Land " arr. G. Hawkins INTERVAL. March ... "Death or Glory" ... R. B. Hall Song "Land of Hope and Glory" Mrs. SHEENA GUISE Selection ... "Village Wedding " ... Sidney Dacre SYNOPSIS : The Courtship; Meet me by Moonlight alone ; Tell me Mary how to woo thee ; Haste to the Wedding ; Church Bells ; Voluntary ; The Ceremony ; Wedding March ; The Toasts ; Dancing on the Green ; At the Ball ; Off she goes ; At Home ; Finale. Song ... ... "Adverts" ... J. G. WILCOX Selection... .. "John Peel" ... J. A. Greenwood Vocal Valse "Flying Trapeze " arr. Gordon Mackenzie Song ... ... "John Willie" ... W. CARDEN Selection... "Sweethearts of Yesterday" Henry Hall Descriptive March ... "Smiling Prince" ... Beechfield Carver "GOD SAVE THE KING."

LIST OF FIXTURES FOR SEASON 1936-37

Date	Fixture	Ground	For	Agst.		Date	Fixture	Ground	For	Agst.
	GENTS.						LADIES.			
Oct. 3	Woking	Home				Sept. 26	Westfield Ladies	Home		
10	Basingstoke	Away				Oct. 3	Wellington Works	Away		
17	R.A.S.C.	Home				10	Thornycrofts	Home		
24	R.H.A.	Away				17	Woking O.S.A.	Away		
31	Alton	Home				24	Odiham Ladies	Home		
Nov. 7	Ascot	Away				31	Reading	Away		
14	Merrow	Home				Nov. 7	Vickers, Ltd.	Home		
21	Courages, Alton	Away				14		Away		
28	Basingstoke	Home				21	Aldershot Town	Home		
Dec. 5	R.A., Ewshott	Away				28	Odiham Ladies	Away		
12	Courages, Alton	Home				Dec. 5		Home		
19	Woking	Away				12	Guildford Banks	Away		
25		Home				19	Traction Co.	Home		
26		Home				26		Away		
1937						28		Away		
Jan. 2	R.A.E.	Home				1937				
9		Away				Jan. 2	Camberley Ladies	Away		
16	Ranelagh Old Boys	Home				9	Wellington Works	Home		
23	R.A.E.	Away				16	Westfield Ladies	Home		
30	2nd Div. Royal Signals	Away				23		Home		
Feb. 6	Merrow	Away				30	Reading	Home		
13	R.A., Ewshott	Home				Feb. 6		Home		
20	Ascot	Away				13	Thornycrofts	Away		
27		Away				20	Aldershot Traction Co.	Away		
Mar. 6	2nd Div. Royal Signals	Away				27	Camberley Ladies	Home		
13	Alton	Away				Mar. 6		Away		
20	R.A.S.C.	Away				13	Woking O.G.A.	Home		
27	R.H.A.	Home				20	Guildford Banks	Home		
April 3	Ranelagh	Away				27		Away		
						April 3	Aldershot High School	Home		

Member's Name

141 Fleet Hockey Club, fixture list, 1936-7. The club was established in 1925 and throughout its existence the cricket ground in Reading Road was the venue for its home matches. In the early days the club ran several strong teams in both the men's and women's sections.

142 Fleet Cricket Club, *c.*1936. Prior to 1904 cricket was played on the ground now occupied by the North Hants Golf Club, but in 1903-4 the club moved to Stockton Avenue. By 1905 the club moved again to its present ground, a lease being granted at a yearly rent of £5 by the Elvetham estate. The group shown includes Hew Pool, Ted Bright, Bill Wright, Stan Wilmot, Len Bourne, George Knowles and Cecil Keene.

Buildings of Note

143 Fleet Mill, Minley Road, *c*.1914. The mill house was timber-framed with brick infilling and the internal partitioning was of wattle and daub. The mill once ground corn using an external waterwheel and is shown on the 1759 map of Hampshire by Isaac Taylor. George Wright was the miller between the 1870s and 1890s and it is believed that the mill last worked in 1940. Since then, after a variety of uses, it fell into disrepair and was recently demolished.

144 Brook House, Crookham Village, *c*.1920-30. The Dutch gable bears the date 1664. The government architect who 'listed' the building considered that it formed a wing of a much larger structure, and foundations have been discovered in the garden and adjacent field to the left. During restoration in the 1960s evidence of a major fire was found. Folklore suggests that Queen Anne and Charles II with Nell Gwynne were past visitors.

145 Crookham House, Church Crookham, was built by Mr. Lefroy in 1861. Originally named 'The Lea', the house was first occupied by the widow of the Rector of Dogmersfield. Subsequent occupants included Lord Frederick Kerr and Sir Richard Moreton. The house was eventually bought by Mr. Stevens of Kent Road and converted into Crookham House Hotel. It was demolished in the 1960s to make way for a housing estate now known as Moreton Close.

146 Stockton House, Fleet, was built *c*.1880. In 1919 the Stockton House estate comprised 32 acres and was described as a small mansion house with stables, farmery and cottages offering potential as a residential hotel or hydro. Sir Seymour Hicks and Lady Hicks (Elaine Terriss) lived here until his death. Thomas Kenward, the local brewer, lived at Stockton House and at one stage also owned Tullamore House, an adjacent property. It now houses a preparatory school.

147 Capital and Counties Bank in Fleet was built in 1889. The photograph shows how imposing the original bank building must have been compared with its surroundings. The ornate stone roof façade and the pedimented red granite porch were removed in 1970 as part of a modernisation programme by Lloyds Bank.

148 Pearsons auction rooms, Fleet, *c*.1910. Many a treasure was sold at one of the weekly sales in the auction rooms in Kings Road. When Pearsons were bought out by Prudential, the building became redundant and was demolished in 1989.

149   The entrance to Basingbourne House, Church Crookham, *c*.1910. Sale details in 1910 reported that the house and gardens occupied nearly 20 acres which included stabling for seven horses, coach-house and paddocks. It described the vicinity as one of the most picturesque and healthy parts of the county. It also said that the 'postal arrangements admit of three collections and three deliveries a day'. Early in the century it was the residence of General Haking, who was G.O.C. of an army corps at Aldershot.

150   A view of the grounds of Basingbourne House from the terrace, *c*.1910. The sale details describe the pleasure gardens and grounds as profusely adorned with specimen conifers and well-grown shrubs. There were tennis and croquet lawns, and in a sheltered situation a very productive fruit and vegetable garden. Basingbourne House, having been divided into flats, is a shadow of its former self.

51 The *Station Hotel*, Fleet, *c*.1910. Built in the last century, the hotel was ideally situated being next to the old Fleet Station and it was still next door when the new station was built. It became *The Fleet Hotel* in the 1950s and was renamed *The Links Hotel* in recent years.

52 Pool & Sons, Fleet Road, *c*.1915. Built about 1913, from a design by H. J. Pool (1848-1939) and Stanley Pool (later County Architect of Cornwall), it was to replace earlier premises at the rear of the Baptist Church in Fleet Road close to the Oatsheaf crossroads. About 1920-21 the entrance to the builder's yard at the rear was closed and a further shop was created. The business then moved to the new site near Fleet Station.

153 Dinorben Court, Church Crookham, *c.*1930. The Galsworthys and Chinnocks lived in Dinorben Court from 1872; Frederick Chinnock was associated with surveyors in London later known as Debenham Chinnock. The property extended to 119 acres and included several cottages, pleasure grounds and gardens. In 1935 the Dinorben Court Estate was sold in 10 lots for development.

154 The dining room at Dinorben Court, *c.*1930. This room had south and east aspects and measured 30 ft. by 18 ft. with panelled wainscotting and oak parquet floor.

155 The Beacon, Fleet, *c.*1915. The Beacon was one of the larger Victorian residences which gave Fleet and District its early genteel character. Early postcards show it as a prominent structure on the crest of the gravel ridge, parallel with and to the north of Reading Road. Buildings of this quality in the area bounded by Reading Road North, Elvetham Road and Fleet Road gave rise to the term the Blue Triangle, with obvious political bias. This term is still used regularly by estate agents today.

156 *The Beacon.* Cover of the hotel brochure. The Beacon opened as a residential hotel in 1946 and was then managed by Miss E. Mercer. It offered full board with lunch for four shillings, tea for one and sixpence and dinner for five shillings. Mr. Stevens, founder of Eriva Dene School, was a co-purchaser of the *Beacon* and was responsible for its change of use to an hotel.

157 Court Moor House, Church Crookham, *c.*1912. Court Moor House stood off the Reading Road South from the mid-19th century until the estate was sold for re-development in 1936. Edgar Figgess was the last occupant. Local builders Pool & Sons retained parts of the building as separate structures and built adjoining properties. The estate occupied the area comprising Linkway, Courtmoor Avenue and Greenways.

158 Ruby Cottage, Albert Street, Fleet, became the offices of the new Fleet Urban District Council in the early part of the century and continued there until 1936-7 when the council, with the adjoining fire station, moved to the Views. From 1937 the whole corner site, including the mortuary and 'Sams' stable, was bought by County Commercial Cars. The building is currently used by Pilgrim Miller, Surveyors and Valuers.

159 Oakley Corner, Fleet. Mr. James Oakley built a shop and house at the corner of Fleet Road and Upper Street and incorporated a clock tower. It became a departmental store, with prestigious royal patronage, selling bicycles, furniture and groceries; it was also an off-licence. The rails on the right-hand side were probably introduced to support an earlier design of awning than that seen on Darracott's shop on the left.

160 The Anchorage, Church Crookham, *c.*1960. In 1910, May's *Fleet Directory* described the building as the Court Moor Home of Rest; it was situated at the corner of Reading Road and Castle Street. The Figgess family of Court Moor House provided the prime support, enabling this home to be built and to function for many years. Eventually it was run by the Church Army and called the Anchorage, finally closing as a home in 1974.

161 Chernocke House, Fleet, *c.*1974. A turn-of-the-century house, occupied until the late 1920s as a doctor's residence and surgery. From the late 1930s it was split into flats and part was used as a Bridge Club. Its final use was as the Public Library, and it was demolished when the present structure, seen behind, was completed in the 1970s.

School Life

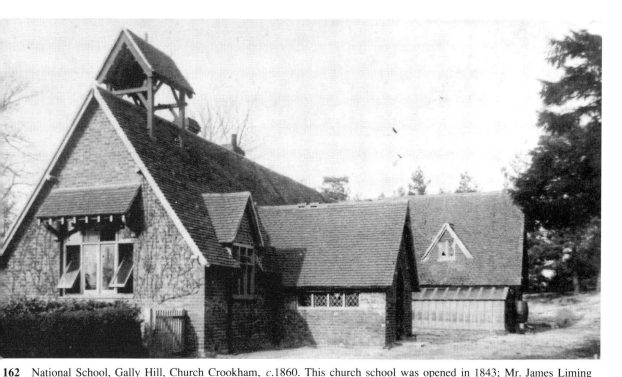

162 National School, Gally Hill, Church Crookham, *c.*1860. This church school was opened in 1843; Mr. James Liming was the first headmaster and Mrs. Stevens the first headmistress. There was one room for the boys and one for the girls, which by 1894 was inadequate. Because of a serious diphtheria epidemic, the building was demolished and a new school was built on the same site.

163 Diphtheria Prevention Certificate, 1944. Diphtheria was particularly feared in the 1940s and the reverse of this certificate explains that, even after the injection, some children quickly lose the protection and any evidence of sore throats should be referred to a doctor.

FLEET URBAN DISTRICT

Diphtheria Prevention Certificate

To the parents of :

Name............FIELD. NOrman, ... Age.........10.

Address.......4, Crookham Street, Crookham.

This is to certify *that the above-named Child has had a Course of Treatment with Diphtheria Prophylactic and is believed to be protected against Diphtheria*

In the event of the Child being ill in the future and your doctor suspecting it to be suffering from Diphtheria, kindly draw his attention to this Certificate, in order that he may acquaint the Medical Officer of Health of the District in which you reside.

(Signed)

Medical Officer of Health.

164 Crookham Church of England School and Headmaster's House, c.1905. This building superseded the National School which opened in 1843 on the same site. Owing to an increase in local population, a separate Infants School was built in the Gally Hill Road in 1911. Both these buildings are still in daily use for infants only. There have only been ten permanent head teachers of the schools on this site during nearly 150 years. The first headmaster, James Liming, served for only eight years but the next, William Davis, stayed for 40 years.

165 The National School, Albert Street, Fleet, c.1905. Mr. Henry Blake sold to the church at half price 18 plots on the corner of Albert Street and Church Road. The school and school house were completed in 1886 at a cost of £858 18s.11d., mostly raised by public subscription. In 1912 the Infant School moved to the new block in Church Road. Until 1947 children remained here for the whole of their school life, at which time Heatherside opened and senior pupils moved out.

166 Staff of Albert Street School, Fleet, *c.*1890. The original staff with Mr. Edwards, schoolmaster, back row, extreme left, Mr. W. Prideaux, headmaster, centre back with his wife seated in front of him. Miss Andrews, extreme right and seated, was the daughter of the station master at Fleet Station. Walter Prideaux remained headmaster until he retired at sixty-five.

167 Giant swing, Albert Street School, *c*.1890. Given by Col. Horniblow, the first chairman of Fleet U.D.C., this giant stride swing for boys was installed in the school playground soon after the school was built.

168 School children, Albert Street School, Fleet, 1902. An early photograph of pupils with Mr. W. Edwards, schoolmaster, on the left.

169 Empire Day, Albert Street School, 1926. Empire Day (24 May) was the only day in the year when the whole school assembled with its Governors. The boys' playground was to the left of the railings, the assembly was on the girls' playground.

170 Prizegiving at Albert Street School, 1929. On Empire Day Dorothy Newell received her prize from Col. Horniblow. He was one of the school managers, as was Billy Parsons, the portly gentleman on the right. He ran the butcher's shop in Fleet Road, near the junction with Church Road. The tall lady was Miss Pulker, the head teacher of the infants' school.

171 Wesleyan Sunday School, Fleet, 1929. In 1929 the school won the shield, presented for one year by *The Methodist Times*, to the school showing the largest percentage increase in scholars. The shield was presented at a public meeting held at the schoolroom by the editor of the *Times*, the Rev. Dr. B. Gregory and Mr. Arthur J. Rank. Mr. H. H. Pool (seated to the right of the shield) became Sunday School Superintendent in 1930.

172　Maypole, Church Crookham, *c.*1928. A garden fête in the grounds of Crookham Vicarage. The church roof line is visible above the trees. This event would have been a repeat of the maypole dance by girls of the Church of England School on Empire Day. The headmaster, A. Dance (1923-31), introduced this celebration which included boys in suits or scout uniforms saluting the flag and girls folk dancing, dressed in white.

173 Eriva Dene School, Fleet, 1960. In 1920, Eric and Eva Stevens, both qualified teachers, opened a private school in Kent Road, using a combination of their Christian names to name the school. Stevens was also involved in property dealing and was associated with the *Beacon* and *Crookham House* hotels. Eriva Dene closed in the early 1970s with 50 pupils.

ERIVA DENE SCHOOL

(Registered School)

CO-EDUCATIONAL DAY SCHOOL

FOUNDED 1923

Boys 4 - 12 years   Girls 4 - 15 years

QUALIFIED STAFF — SMALL CLASSES

Principal:

MR. E. M. STEVENS, B.A., INTER.B.SC.

Full-time Assistants:

MRS. SEARLE, L.R.A.M.

MRS. SMITH, B. OF EDUC. CERT.

MISS GERRARD, *Kindergarten*

Visiting Dancing, Art and Games Teachers

— — — — — — — — — — — — —

Tuition Fees: £10 10s. 0d. per term

— — — — — — — — — — — — —

17 Kent Road

FLEET : HANTS

174 St Nicholas School, Fleet, a private school, was established in 1937 through the combined efforts of Miss Helen Pritchard and Miss Angela McKenzie. Two years earlier they had bought Pinehurst, nearby in Branksomewood Road, but this was soon outgrown. Renamed St Nicholas after the patron saint for children, the school developed strongly after the war and other properties were acquired to allow for expansion.

175 The music room at St Nicholas School, post 1974. One of a series of pictures of various rooms in the school, including the drawing room, a classroom and a dormitory. The music room is in School House, a building on the west side of Branksomewood Road.

Bibliography

Baigent, F. J., *The Crondal Records* (1891)

Butterfield, R. P., *Monastery and Manor, The History of Crondall* (1948)

Edwards, A. G., *Fleet—The Town of My Youth*, Rev. ed. (1993)

Evans, J. and Garland, P., *Christ Church and the Parish of Crookham* (1991)

Hampshire County Council, 'Hampshire Treasures Survey', Vol. 3, Hart and Rushmoor (1979)

Kelly's Directories, Fleet & Crookham, pre-1900

May's Directories, Fleet & Crookham, 1910-1950

Meirion-Jones, G. I., *All Saints Church, Fleet 1862-1987* (1987)

Page, W., *V.C.H. of Hampshire*, Part 33, Crondall Hundred (1911)

Roe, E., *Old Fleet and Crookham* (1975)

Stooks, C. D., *History of Crondall & Yateley* (1905)